*Masters of Equitation
on Canter*

Masters of Equitation on Canter

Compiled by
Martin Diggle

J. A. Allen
London

© Martin Diggle 2001
First Published in Great Britain 2001

ISBN 0 85131 812 6

J. A. Allen
Clerkenwell House
Clerkenwell Green
London EC1R 0HT

J. A. Allen is an imprint of Robert Hale Ltd

British Library Cataloguing in Publication Data
A catalogue record for this book is available from the British Library

All extracts from *Dressage A Study of the Finer Points of Riding* by Henry Wynmalen
are reproduced by permission of the Wilshire Book Company (California, USA);
from *Riding Logic* by Wilhelm Müseler by permission of The Random House
Group Ltd.; from *The Complete Training of Horse and Rider* by Alois Podhajsky by
permission of The Sportsman's Press; from *The Gymnasium of the Horse* by Gustav
Steinbrecht by permission of Xenophon Press (Cleveland Heights, Ohio, USA).

The following photographs and illustrations are also reproduced by permission:
Sequence of steps at the canter (page 20) and Young horse at the canter (page 25)
from Podhajsky's *The Complete Training of Horse and Rider* by permission of The
Sportsman's Press; Frl. von Opel on Arnim (page 33) and Position right (page 62),
from Müseler's *Riding Logic* by permission of The Random House Group Ltd.;
Outward signs of tractability and insufficient tractability (page 82) from Knopfhart's
Dressage A Guidebook for the Road to Success by permission of Half Halt Press, Inc.
(PO Box 67, Boonsboro, Maryland 21756, USA).

Jacket photograph of the compiler by permission of Mike Freeman

The compiler and publisher acknowledge all of these generous permissions with
thanks. Despite our best efforts we have been unable to trace ownership of the
copyright of some material included in this book. If anyone feels that they have a
claim, please contact the publisher.

Design by Nancy Lawrence
Series compiler Martin Diggle
Printed in Hong Kong

Contents

Introduction to the Masters of Equitation on Dressage Series

When we first discover a new pursuit, most of us explore it with more enthusiasm than science. This is necessarily so, since our desire to participate greatly exceeds our understanding of the principles involved. It is when we begin actively to seek a greater understanding of these principles that we can be sure that we have acquired a genuine new interest, and are not simply indulging a passing fad.

In our quest for knowledge, we look first to the nearest and most obvious sources. If our new interest is riding, we acquire an instructor, listen (hopefully) to what we are told, and begin to question the apparent paradoxes of equitation as they unfold. With time, our field of information broadens; we learn what our instructor has been told by his or her instructor, we begin to follow the exploits of top riders in the different disciplines, and we even start to read books.

It is at some point along this path that we start to realise just what a wealth of knowledge we have at our disposal. We also begin to realise that much of this knowledge is far from new. There is initial surprise when we learn that the elderly gentleman who trains our current idol was, himself, an Olympic medallist – a further surprise that he, in turn, was trained by a cavalry officer famed, in his time, as a leading light of the Cadre Noir. We discover in a book written forty or fifty years ago ideas of which we were unaware, and then marvel at the extensive references to writers long dead before the author's own birth. We regard, with awe, faded, grainy photographs of riders whose positions – even to our untutored eyes – look positively centaur-like, and we are bemused by ancient diagrams of school movements that make today's dressage tests seem like a hack in the park.

If, at this point, we pause to reflect a little, we start to see this heritage in its true context. It is a common human conceit to believe that we, or our near contemporaries, are the first to discover anything, but this is very rarely true. So far as riding is concerned, it is no exaggeration to say that it is, in absolute terms, less important to us than it was to our ancestors. If we need to prove this point we can consider that, three hundred years ago, a poorly ridden lateral movement might result in decapitation by an enemy sabre. The same movement, ridden today, would result in an 'insufficient' on the test sheet, and a wounded ego.

Of course, it is not the case that all equitation of times past was concerned with the vital necessities of war. Certainly since the renaissance, there have always been people fascinated by the art of riding – interestingly, this group includes a number of Masters who were, first and foremost, military men.

It is in the nature of art to give birth to experimentation, innovation and re-interpretation, and it is in the nature of artists to be influenced by – even to borrow from – others, and yet still develop their own styles. Sometimes, in pursuit of new ideas, an acknowledged Master may stray too far down a particular path, causing even his most admiring pupils to question the wisdom of the route, but such instances have a way of triggering the reassessment and consolidation of major principles.

All of these things have happened in equitation, against a background of different types and breeds of horses, and varying equestrian requirements. Not surprisingly, this has given rise to a number of schools, or philosophies, which place different degrees of emphasis on certain principles. By delving into the wealth of literature available, it is possible for the avid reader to discover these philosophies, and draw from them ideas and information which may be of personal value. However, because of the amount of material available, and the need to embark upon a major voyage of discovery, this can be considered an extensive - albeit rewarding – process.

The purpose behind the *Masters of Equitation* series is to gather together, under individual subject headings, many of the key thoughts of eminent equestrians, thus providing a convenient source of reference to their ideas. The reader is invited to research, compare and contrast – and may find a special significance in areas of obvious consensus.

Compiler's Note

In producing this series of books, the aims of the publisher are twofold. First, it is certainly the intention that they should act as reference works, giving readers with specific schooling queries access to the thoughts of many Masters in a single volume.

Second, it is very much hoped that they will act as an appetiser, a stimulus for further reading of the original works cited and, indeed, for Classical equestrian works in general.

With regard to this latter aim, I can foresee that some readers, who have already made a study of the Classics, may search this book in vain for their favourite extract or author. If this happens, I beg such readers' pardon. The truth is, in order to be completely comprehensive, a book such as this would have to quote great swathes of material from very many sources – an undertaking that would exhaust the energies of compiler, publisher and perhaps even the most ardent reader!

Rather than attempt the impossible, I have endeavoured to provide in this series a good cross-section of references from different eras, countries and schools of equestrian thought. It was, indeed, the publisher's express wish that the series should contain a broad overview of various ideas and persuasions and that it should not seek to promote the ideas of one School over another. Some of the quoted material comes from writers who may not be instantly recognised as pre-eminent 'Masters'; these extracts are included for reasons of interest or contrast, or simply because they are apposite.

For those who would welcome a rationale for the material included and omitted, I will attempt to provide one in a brief historical context.

In the first instance, there are no extracts from Xenophon's *The Art of Horsemanship*. By way of explanation, I can do no better than quote from W. Sidney Felton's excellent work, *Masters of Equitation:*

Xenophon's approach to schooling [his humane understanding of the horse] makes it easy to see why he is widely quoted by modern writers on equitation. Indeed, it would seem that many authors feel that they have not adequately established a claim to a knowledge of classical equitation if they do not find an opportunity to refer to Xenophon as the first master of the art of riding...However, in honoring Xenophon as the earliest and hence one of the most significant of a long series of writers on the subject of equitation, we must not lose sight of the fact that educated riding as it exists today has been built up from the contributions of a long line of skilled horsemen over a long period of years. It is remarkable that Xenophon should have expressed so clearly the principles that should govern our approach to...schooling... the horse, but we should not make the mistake of asserting that he was also the master of techniques of riding that did not even come into existence until many centuries after his era.

I should add that I have great personal admiration for Xenophon's humanity and understanding of the horse's psyche, which I believe were not equalled until well beyond the renaissance era. Which brings us to that era, and my reasons for the paucity of quotations from it.

With no evidence to the contrary, it is generally accepted that, throughout the Dark Ages and the medieval period, equitation, in the modern sense, did not exist. Horses were basically compelled to do their riders' bidding, by whatever brutal means were most expedient. The rise, in sixteenth century Italy, of the Neapolitan School, saw the *beginning* of a remarkable change. My reason for emphasising *beginning* is that the renaissance in riding should be seen in the literal sense of the word, a 'rebirth'. To illustrate this point, when Federigo Grisone, the founder of the Neapolitan School, emphasised the importance of the rider's legs in schooling, his suggestion was seized upon as a great innovation and refinement of what had gone before.

It is certainly true that teachers of the School, such as Grisone, Fiaschi and Pignatelli introduced the concept of riding as a science and an art and their influence 'lit the fuse', as it were, for the explosion of equestrian thought that was to follow. However, while their influence (especially that of Pignatelli, through his illustrious pupils from many countries) was immense, the Neapolitan School can be seen as instigating an awakening from the Dark Ages which was both gradual and prolonged. Snapshots of this School are provided, again, by W. Sidney Felton:

What was this new type of riding and schooling which gained such rapid acceptance? First of all, it was a method based on complete subjugation of the horse. Training was often carried on not by one person alone, but by a riding master with one, two or even more assistants. All of these assistants carried whips or rods. And from the short length of time that a whip was reported as lasting, it is evident that they were not merely pointed at the horse...[as] in longeing.

13

A great deal of work was done with pillars, that is the horse was fastened to a single pillar and worked in a circle around it.

Curb bits were used exclusively and were of a most elaborate design. The riders of that day...had an infinite variety of designs. But all of these bits without exception had one thing in common – that they had very long cheeks and were very severe by any modern standard. And the effect is clearly seen in the pictures illustrating what was then considered proper carriage and proper action, for in our eyes the horses were very much overcollected. Again and again we see horses pictured with their heads as much as thirty degrees behind the vertical and quite apparently behind the bit.

Perhaps it is an unfair inference, but one cannot but wonder whether the horsemen of this period were not afraid of their horses. Certainly they used every possible method of restraint, and extended gaits or even a free...walk on a loose rein had no place in their schooling.

If these reflections seem, to modern readers, to be damning, the writer goes on to make a telling point:

But, while we may find much in the early school riding which we would not wish to follow today, we must not lose sight of the fact that it represented a great step forward from anything which had preceded it...and that it was the foundation for the more modern school riding, particularly in France, which in turn has become the advanced dressage riding of today.

It is likely that several factors contributed to the decline of the Neapolitan School and the ascendancy of the French School. W. Sidney Felton adds his own theory that the early form of School riding...

...had relatively little utilitarian value. It was a very specialized sport or game developed partly for the gratification of the participant but very largely for its spectator appeal. The French Court...provided a much grander stage...than was available in the small [and often warring] Italian principalities...

Two of the founder figures of the French School were Salomon de la Broue and Antoine de Pluvinel, both of whom had studied at the Neapolitan School. De la Broue was the first trainer of his era to use a bridoon rather than a curb bit in the early stages of training. De Pluvinel, a student of Pignatelli, is credited with being the first humane trainer of his era. Although this should be considered in the context of his times, he certainly took account of the horse's powers of reasoning, and understood that the horse does not always resist out of malice, but frequently through lack of understanding.

De Pluvinel was also riding instructor to King Louis XIII, and it was his success, together with that of de la Broue, which caused the French Monarchy to give its support to equitation, founding the School of Versailles, which flourished until the French Revolution. It was this background that produced the figure widely regarded as the most influential in the history of equitation, François Robichon de la Guérinière. W. Sidney Felton describes him thus:

We come now, in the first half of the eighteenth century, to the man who has often been described as the greatest horseman of all time. De la Guérinière, building on the foundation established by de Pluvinel, accomplished what was little short of a revolution. He initiated that artistic freedom of action which is so characteristic of the modern French School and he developed the methods by which that freedom could be obtained...We might fairly call him the first of the modern classical riders. His book,

Ecole de Cavalerie, though published in 1733, is still considered a standard work and is often quoted by students of equitation.

Of course, it is now a very long time since de la Guérinière was writing and teaching. The art and science of equitation have continued to develop on an increasingly international basis, and many great Masters have appeared since his time. For the most part, it is extracts from their works which feature in these pages. It seems to me that de la Guérinière represents a fundamental watershed in equestrian history, and his abiding influence on Classical equitation is the main reason why most of the quotations in this series are 'post-Guérinière'.

One final point, concerning form of words. The Masters quoted in this book wrote in various eras, languages and styles and, in many cases, their work has been subject to translation. Therefore, the reader may notice that word forms and usage appear to vary from one extract to another. Other than this, variations in actual spellings are a consequence of quoting verbatim from English and American publications.

Introduction to the Masters of Equitation on Canter

Canter is the most complex of the school gaits, and, when carried out well, the most expressive and impressive. It is the gait from which, in its finished form, movements such as tempi changes, zigzags and pirouettes are produced.

Because of its complexity, it is essential that due consideration is given to the quality of the gait at each stage of its development. Rushed or careless work will seriously compromise the gait, and advanced movements – if they can be produced at all – will be forced travesties, lacking elegance and grace.

In this book, various Masters give their thoughts on the introduction and correct development of the basic gait. Their thoughts on collecting and lengthening the canter, lateral work and counter-canter and changes of lead will be subject matter for further titles in this series.

Readers unfamiliar with the usage should note that many European writers have traditionally used the French *galop* (which serves for both canter and gallop) when referring to the three-beat gait of canter. This, in many instances, has been rendered as 'gallop' in translations – some examples of which appear in the following pages.

The Value of Canter

Since many riders feel that a correct, balanced canter is the most pleasant gait to ride, it would perhaps be appropriate to begin this book with a reference to the aesthetic value of the gait from one of the greatest of the Masters:

The canter, or school gallop, is a gallop which is regular, collected, shortened in the forehand and powerful at the quarters...it does not drag the hindquarters along, as it were; and produces as a result of balance in the horse that beautiful cadence which charms the spectator as greatly as it pleases the rider.

François Robichon de la Guérinière *School of Horsemanship*

Gustav Steinbrecht was a great advocate of forward movement, and a stern critic of those he believed to stress 'lightness' and collection at the expense of this quality. Here is a quotation that expresses this perfectly, and takes equitation out of the boundaries of the arena and into a wider context:

Nevertheless, it cannot be denied that an impulsive canter is the main prerequisite for a good riding horse, not only for a soldier or the hunt or the race rider, but also for those who ride for pleasure. The canter is preferred if the rider's comfort must be considered, for example for older people or persons of ill health.

And it is justified on the promenade where one wishes to present the most advantageous picture and wishes to hold unconstrained conversations.

He continues:

The selection of a riding horse will therefore most certainly be based on a special test of its natural canter, particularly since innate deficiencies in this gait, just as in walk, cannot be completely eradicated even by the most careful dressage training.

And:

Count Lehndorf is still correct today [mid nineteenth century], writing in his book about horse breeding, that here in Germany, when we evaluate horses, we pay too much attention to the trot, a mistake not made by the practical Englishman.

Gustav Steinbrecht *The Gymnasium of the Horse*

Sequence of steps at the canter. From Podhajsky's
The Complete Training of Horse and Rider.

While Lt. Col. d'Endrödy's view of canter remarks upon both the aesthetic and practical qualities of the gait:

The canter is a soft, rhythmical pace, and its rocking-like movements can be followed agreeably by the rider. Among all the paces, the swinging movement of the horse's back is most pronounced in the canter. Because of this natural quality, the canter can be of substantial help during the horse's schooling in developing its back action.

Lt. Col. A.L. d'Endrödy *Give Your Horse a Chance*

Introducing the Canter

There are, basically, two schools of thought regarding the introduction of canter under saddle. The first, which tends to represent the older Classical view, is that the horse's education (and thus his balance, suppleness and obedience) should be fairly advanced before any canter work is attempted – the aim being to obtain a good gait from the outset. The second school, which becomes more prevalent in relatively modern times, does not deny the basic virtues of the first. It does, however, attach certain schooling advantages to the relatively early introduction of canter – provided that this is done with due discretion. The ethos of this school might be summarised as *allowing* canter, where appropriate, and benefiting from its influence on longitudinal suppleness and impulsion. As with so much in equitation, it is perhaps most constructive to view these approaches as alternative, rather than opposing, schools of thought.

Like most of the older Masters, de la Guérinière believed that horses should be at quite an advanced stage of schooling before being asked to canter. The preparatory work he describes would, of course be beneficial – the piaffe between the pillars helping to strengthen the hindquarters. Shoulder-in, the exercise he developed, is mentioned overtly for its primary role – suppling – but it is evident that de la Guérinière also appreciated its value in preventing/correcting crookedness in canter.

It is a principle to which all experienced masters subscribe that a horse should never be galloped before having been suppled with the trot so that it neither bears on the hands nor pulls at the reins. One must wait, then, until the horse is supple in its entire body, trained to the shoulder-in and the croup to the wall, and is accomplished in the piaffe between the pillars; and as soon as it has reached this point of development, it will perform the gallop willingly and without much coaxing.

François Robichon de la Guérinière *School of Horsemanship*

It is interesting to see the general principles outlined by de la Guérinière echoed, over a century and a half later by an Englishman working in Europe and Russia…

I never begin the canter before getting the horse thoroughly under control, by which I mean that he should be physically, and, if I may say, morally obedient to me…I expect, above all things, the loins, haunches and hocks to be perfectly supple…in order that I may be able to utilize the resulting forces as I wish.

Having obtained these conditions, I am certain to presently succeed in placing my horse in a proper position for the canter, and to immediately get the canter I wish the horse to do, and not the one he desires to perform.

If the horse obeys the legs, I shall be able to prevent him from going *sideways,* which is an extremely bad habit, and which is better to prevent than to punish. It is much more difficult to straighten a horse which is accustomed to throw his hind quarters to the right or left, than to teach him to canter straight from the beginning. James Fillis *Breaking and Riding*

…and a further half-century on by an all-round horseman domiciled in England:

The same reasons that make it difficult for the rider to ride correctly at canter, make it difficult for an unschooled horse to go correctly at this pace, and quite impossible for any rider, however good or expert he may be, to make him do so. And that is the reason why all schooling at the canter ought to be left to form the last part of the horse's education. If we canter him too early we shall not be able to obtain an easy and nicely balanced pace, but be likely to create bad habits, such as plunging or head-throwing, which we might have great difficulty in correcting later on.

On the other hand, when a horse has first been carefully balanced, suppled, collected and made obedient to the legs, we shall be able to obtain a good canter, with balance and collection, almost at once.   Henry Wynmalen *Equitation*

The significance of the phrase 'almost at once' becomes apparent when this author discusses the practicalities of introducing canter, since it seems clear that, even after extensive preparation, Wynmalen does not expect perfection straight away.

I do not expect collection or absolute evenness of pace during the first few days, and do not take too much notice of the way he carries his head. If we ask too much at once we shall but confuse and excite the horse, which is exactly what we should avoid.
                                         Henry Wynmalen *Equitation*

The American Olympic rider John Winnett is a great devotee of de la Guérinière, and his own views on introducing canter contain a quote from the old Master:

Canter training should not start until the end of the first phase of training, or indeed, until the horse is supple, strong and balanced in the trot. If 'the utility of the walk is the necessity of the trot' [de la Guérinière], then 'the quality of the trot is reflected in the canter!'.   John Winnett *Dressage as Art in Competition*

These views on the preparation required for canter are supported in general terms by Alois Podhajsky...

When work at the walk and trot has been established, but not before, *work at the canter* may begin.
    Alois Podhajsky *The Complete Training of Horse and Rider*

Young horse at the canter. From Podhajsky's
The Complete Training of Horse and Rider.

...and, essentially, by another Director of the Spanish Riding School, Kurt Albrecht – although his second sentence perhaps suggests a willingness to introduce canter at a somewhat earlier stage than the preceding writers.

Of course, the canter is not a suitable gait for the initial stages of schooling; the horse's hind limbs are not yet strong enough and the firm leg pressures needed to sustain the gait can alarm the horse. However, once the horse accepts the aid of the legs without fuss and remains in balance when the rider sits to the trot, the canter can be introduced for short periods of time.

Kurt Albrecht *Principles of Dressage*

Richard Wätjen on the five-year-old Tolerant, working canter left. From Wätjen's Dressage Riding.

Richard Wätjen says much the same as Podhajsky and Albrecht...

If the horse is well on the bit at the walk and trot the rider can start with the work at the canter.

...whilst warning against any impatience in reaching this stage:

The rider should not hurry in any way when teaching his horse to canter, for the more obedient it is at the walk and trot, and the more it has learned to relax under its rider, the easier will it accept the aids for striking off and maintaining the canter.

Richard Wätjen *Dressage Riding*

Writing in the latter part of the nineteenth century, Gustav Steinbrecht was perhaps one of the first Masters to advocate the relatively early introduction of canter. On the topic of schooling young horses he wrote:

Although the trot must always be practiced with priority, the canter should by no means be excluded since it is a quite natural gait which requires the greatest thrust and impulsion from the haunches, like a jump. It is therefore an exaggerated caution to want to exclude this gait as an exercise as soon as the stimulation and development of the forward driving forces of the hindquarters are involved. We have also had it confirmed in practice that for slow horses extensive exercises at a fast canter enable them to produce a deliberate trot much more easily and faster than by unchanging, tiring trot exercises.

Gustav Steinbrecht *The Gymnasium of the Horse*

It is very clear, however, that Steinbrecht considered initial canter work as a *useful adjunct* of early schooling, to be introduced with due discretion:

It is not advisable, however, to force young horses to canter, at least not in the arena where they are required to perform regular turns. In the horse's natural carriage the canter is a rather free and lively gait which requires a certain flexibility to travel through four corners. Clumsy or very inflexible horses must first be prepared for these turns in the quiet gaits...Continuous straight lines in an open field do not require this consideration for turns. Gustav Steinbrecht *The Gymnasium of the Horse*

As a young man, Steinbrecht had studied veterinary medicine. His veterinary knowledge comes to the fore when he elaborates on the need for a judicious approach to early canter work.

Mentioning the dangers to the soundness of their limbs inherent in premature or faulty use of the canter in young horses, the reasons that force us to restrain ourselves during the first canter should be discussed in greater detail. Although it is undoubtedly correct that the horse's natural canter has the advantage of developing the greatest thrust, this fact and the footfalls inherent to this gait...also result in increased wear of the limbs. The body weight is thrown to the forehand with much impulsion, until the inside hind leg participates sufficiently in carrying the load. The forelegs are thus used increasingly as support and are stressed slightly. This becomes particularly apparent in all turns in the arena, that is, when riding through the four corners...Consequently, we must first exclude the canter during the initial training phase for horses that do not carry themselves sufficiently in natural balance...and use it only after we have given them, through trot work, the necessary self-carriage and thus the ability to carry the load primarily on the hind legs. Second, we must avoid tight turns in the first canter exercises and therefore use either continuous straight lines or a large circle...
Gustav Steinbrecht *The Gymnasium of the Horse*

However:

If these facts and recommendations are considered the canter may also be very useful in the earliest stages of training since it is the fastest way to cause the young horse to willingly yield its back muscles, takes away its barn freshness and prevents it from being foolish. All of these goals are also attained with much less effort on the part of the rider than in continuous trot work. Early canter work with young horses may therefore considerably facilitate and accelerate their training.

Gustav Steinbrecht *The Gymnasium of the Horse*

Like most experienced trainers, Steinbrecht appreciated the value of 'listening to the horse'. In summing up the pros and cons of early canter work, he offers the following guidance:

It has already been pointed out that the canter can be of use in the first phase of the horse's training where the preferred goal is the development of thrust into the hands. This gait, in particular, has the advantage that it best develops this force. On the other hand, a warning was also given not to force the young horse to change to the canter, particularly in the arena where they must continuously perform turns. From the advice given there not to interfere with the young, talented horse if it selects canter for itself we can also draw the conclusion that the greater or lesser willingness with which the horse takes up the canter is always the most reliable yardstick for when we can use the canter without doing damage. Conformation and temperament of the horse will be the primary determining factors.

Gustav Steinbrecht *The Gymnasium of the Horse*

His summing up of the whole issue both highlights his novel thinking and puts it firmly into context:

After these…remarks we want to generally comment on the canter question with respect to two…roughly opposite opinions. We can initially admit that the teaching of earlier times, according to which a young horse was allowed to canter only after it had found its perfect balance in the walk and trot, can now be considered old-fashioned. On the other hand, we must qualify the statement that early canter exercises are extremely useful…to be accurate only conditionally. For systematic dressage training the trot offers such great advantages that it will probably always remain its main gait.

Gustav Steinbrecht *The Gymnasium of the Horse*

Waldemar Seunig, who shared Steinbrecht's general philosophy, had a remarkably laissez-faire attitude to young horses who voluntarily offer canter…

…Should the horse when in open terrain break into a canter of his own accord, it should be accepted thankfully at this stage of training… Waldemar Seunig *The Essence of Horsemanship*

…and explained how the impulsion generated may benefit the trot. Like many European trainers of his era, he used the term 'gallop' (French: *galop*) for canter.

Once the horse has acquired the necessary suppleness and power in its hindquarters and back, it will commence to gallop [canter] by itself. The rider can accept this gait without concern, rounding the corners possibly even more than at the trot. At such a voluntary gait, which is merely the manifestation of an animation that cannot be overesteemed, the horse will be able to carry itself without difficulty, since it is merely doing what it likes to do and what offers no difficulty, except at moments of excitement and convulsiveness which we are able to avoid in the present case. That is why we allow it to gallop along until it returns to the trot by itself. This trot will have gained in flow and impulsion.

Waldemar Seunig *Horsemanship*

Later in the same book, Seunig puts his thoughts into more detailed context, making a very specific distinction between allowing and compelling:

We have already discussed the reasons for and against early galloping. It is our principle that the gallop should not be repressed when spontaneously offered, though still less should we try to compel the horse to gallop in the riding hall if it is unable as yet to maintain its poise. At the outset it will be difficult for a remount whose whole configuration is not that of an inherently balanced horse to keep its balance at gallop. But after a few weeks or months so much progress will have been made in its physical development and...balance that we can readily let such a horse slide into a *working gallop* almost without its becoming aware of it. Previously we might have had to force it to gallop, but that would have given it such a dislike for the gait that it would have laid back its ears and manifested tension at every gallop depart.

If galloped too early in the riding hall, a horse without poise would begin to hurry and run away, so that the rider would have to use restraining controls willy-nilly to hold it down and thus impair all its training.

But this does not mean that a young, spirited horse...should not be galloped to relax it and place it under control out in the open, on long straightaways, where there is no need to use the hand held low to exert a restraining action. On the contrary, if we try pedantically to hold such a horse back...while it longs for free leaps on springy meadow ground, such a struggle with its mouth will do much more harm...than it could cause by itself in making a few youthful forward capers...

What is most important in these occasional galloping exercises is that the horse should take them as something natural and a matter of course rather than as an exciting event.

The time to let the horse discover the *correct gallop on a large circle* in the riding hall will have come when it is able to carry itself in a shortened working trot and can obey the lateral controls.

Waldemar Seunig *Horsemanship*

Col. Mylius on Cottstown; natural gallop without reins.
From Seunig's Horsemanship.

Frl. von Opel on Arnim; working canter left with loose reins.
From Müseler's Riding Logic.

In his other book, *The Essence of Horsemanship,* Seunig is unequivocal in stating the schooling value of what he describes as 'the natural canter'...

...the counterpart of the natural trot...
Purpose: To loosen, to have the horse accept the bit confidently, to awaken his impulsion to encourage the suppleness of his back, to keep him fresh, to improve steady contact, to quieten, to educate in relaxation and 'giving', to accustom the horse to remain on the chosen leg. Achievement of a balanced carriage without seeking to use the reins as a 'fifth leg'.

...and recommending:

Very soon after the initial schooling introduce the horse to this gait, on straight lines, in open country, on a sandy or otherwise smooth and springy ground. Next to 'free' jumping or turns on the forehand, this is the best method by which to eliminate all tenseness and thus make the horse supple and prepare him to move freely on the aids. The canter must not be regarded by the horse as a 'special event'.

Waldemar Seunig   *The Essence of Horsemanship*

Multiple Olympic medallist André Jousseaume shared the view that, while the horse should not be *trained* as such in the early stages of canter, there was value in using the gait for suppling purposes:

The horse will be cantered with the neck kept long; but the training at this gait will not really begin until the following period.

However, if the horse is well balanced, not heavy and fairly supple, he can be worked at the canter on a large circle at one end of the riding school, increasing and decreasing the diameter. This work is an excellent suppling exercise.

André Jousseaume   *Progressive Dressage*

A view on the introduction of canter which might be described as balanced and cautious is provided by Reiner Klimke:

The canter...should not be asked for until the young horse is truly accepting the rider's aids in trot. We do not, of course, stop the horse from cantering if it feels like it, either in the arena or when hacking out. On the other hand, it should not be forced to canter as most horses find it easier to carry themselves in the trot. We also have to make the horse familiar with the aids for cantering otherwise it is apt to rush forward and we then have to correct it by pulling at the reins.

Reiner Klimke *Basic Training of the Young Horse*

Ruth Klimke on Optomist. From Klimke's
Basic Training of the Young Horse.

The Canter Aids

It becomes apparent quite early in a rider's career that there is more than one way of producing a transition into canter. Which method is correct? All riders have their theories, and many Masters provide lucid explanations of their own practices. The late Portuguese Maestro, Nuno Oliveira, has an interesting comment on this issue:

The way in which the strike off at the canter should be done has been the subject of innumerable controversies.

The Comte d'Aure provoked the strike off at the canter to the right by using his left leg, after having slightly turned the horse's hindquarters to the right by employing the left rein.

Baucher, in his first method, used diagonal aids. His example was followed by James Fillis, and by nearly all the *écuyers* of that time. But, at the end of his career, Baucher finished by using interior lateral aids.

Each one of these ways is good. The most essential thing is to give the horse the appropriate gymnastic preparation in order to strike off in the canter by pre-determined aids.

Nuno Oliveira *Reflections on Equestrian Art*

A certain irony lies behind Oliveira's reference to Baucher. François Baucher was a man well used to attacks from those who opposed his views, and often replied in kind. The following is the start of a scathing attack on those who, in his view, had created confusion over the transition to canter on a named lead:

> What contrary opinions upon the means to employ to make the horse go off with his right foot? It is the support of the rider's right leg which determines the movement, one pretends; it is that of the left leg, says another; it is the equal touch of the two legs, affirms a third; no, some others remark, very seriously, you must let the horse act naturally.
>
> François Baucher *New Method of Horsemanship* (in *François Baucher, the Man and his Method*, by Hilda Nelson)

It is doubtless true that the various methods he reported were all in force. His own view was that the correct positioning of the horse prior to canter was of more consequence than the actual aids. This view was shared and expounded by several eminent followers of Baucher, including General L'Hotte, who wrote:

> D'Aure, with his extensive experience, and Baucher, who attempted the most complicated movements, neither one...regulated their actions on the motion of the horse's limbs. In equitation, it is not a question of refining or following minutely the horse when he raises or puts down each of his limbs, or of regulating one's actions on one or other of these fleeting actions. One must look at art with a wider perspective, otherwise one will follow a path filled with difficulties, already so numerous and inherent in equitation.
>
> It is the same when striking off at the canter on a specific leg, based on which one is put down, as established by Aubert [P-A Aubert, professor of equitation and equerry of the Ecole Royale d'Application, who wrote a critique of Baucher's methods]. Aubert wants the striking off at the canter on the right leg to be determined the moment the left hindleg is placed on the ground.

This is what Aubert calls 'seizing the leg at the right moment'. Thus the placing down of the leg must, at the same time, be felt by the rider who must be sufficiently skilled with his hand and legs to put them, at that very moment, into play, in accord with its being raised at the canter. The obedience of the horse must be instantaneous otherwise the right moment, that is, the moment of the leg, is lost.

What demands are to be satisfied during so fleeting an instant when the leg is in contact with the ground!...

When one is dealing with Classical or *savante* equitation, there are certain movements which require a great deal of precision in determining how they are to be used. This precision can correspond to the motion of the limbs, but it is not the motion that regulates our actions. It is the position that the horse takes in general and whose leg motion is only the consequence which guides us and makes us sense when our aids must act.

This is also the case with lead changes in general. To achieve this, one must follow a progressive pattern. In principle, a lead change is not obtained as soon as the requested position is given. The same holds true of the striking off at the canter. One must wait for the horse, for it is he who executes the movement.

Alexis-François L'Hotte   *Questions Équestres*

L'Hotte goes on to discuss this issue using Baucher's terminology of 'forces' (in effect, the horse's strength/energy) and 'contractions' (inappropriate muscular tension):

Instead of attempting to regulate his actions based on the motion of the limbs, the *écuyer* will find a whole gamut of studies that are interesting and fertile, by applying himself to perfect the position, that is, the combination of forces and, as such, the distribution of mass that is correct for each movement. In order to be able to destroy quickly resistances which could oppose the correct position and bring about the use of forces to assure accuracy, the *écuyer* must try to acquire the feeling of contractions. In order to put this feeling into evidence and to make its value appreciated, I will, for example, take the horse who, when asked to canter on the right lead, responds by a combination of forces and canters on the left lead.

The rider who lacks any equestrian feeling can only know when the canter is on the determined lead by means of his eyes. The rider who can feel the horse through his seat, after two or three strides at the canter, is able to determine whether the horse took off on the left lead. The judicious horseman with sufficient equestrian tact will be able to appreciate the position from which the canter on the left lead emanated, will rectify it and, before provoking the strike-off, will replace it by the correct position for canter on the right lead. The écuyer who has a feeling for contractions will not have to rectify the false position in that he will not let it occur. He will prevent it from happening by combating, at the very outset, the contractions brought about by the false position and replace those that bring about the correct position at the strike-off at the canter on the right lead.

Alexis-François L'Hotte *Questions Équestres*

Another writer who emphasised the fundamental importance of positioning was the Hungarian-born all-round horseman, Lt. Col. d'Endrödy:

The most appropriate moment for the strike-off is when the hind leg which is on the side opposite to the direction of the canter (the outside leg) and the foreleg which will 'lead' the movement (the inside leg) are in support position. This particular position occurs in walk and in trot during the corresponding diagonal phase of the pace. For instance, if the object is to bring the horse into a canter to the left, the signal for the strike-off should be given when the animal is in its left diagonal support phase.

In a stationary position the horse is completely supported by all four legs; consequently, it can start the movement immediately by striking off on either of its forelegs.

Owing to the fact that there are two diagonal support phases in the same stride, the horse has two opportunities to execute the strike-off during each stride, either to the right or to the left. In spite of this twofold possibility, it will never hesitate in its choice, but will select for its action the direction which best suits the general *position* of its body.

Therefore, before making any attempt to execute the task, the rider should first place the horse in the position which corresponds to the direction of the canter action he wishes to perform. Thus the principal 'aid' for the execution of the action is to create the proper position. If the rider *aids* the animal into this position and then signals the action he requires, the horse will fulfil his demand accordingly and without hesitation. This is why it is impossible to propose the strict application of any special 'aid' for the purpose. There is only one rule, but it is most important: the horse must be *struck off* into canter, and not *driven* into it.

The position of the horse for the strike-off is correct: when it is straight, or bent in the direction of the strike-off action, and the lateral mobility of the shoulders is unobstructed.

Lt. Col. A.L. d'Endrödy *Give Your Horse A Chance*

However, General Decarpentry (a grandson of a pupil of Baucher's, and one of equitation's greatest thinkers), did not entirely share this view. Whilst he certainly appreciated the *value* of correct positioning for canter, he did not see it as the whole answer, as this extract from *Academic Equitation* shows:

From the time of Xenophon, the problem of striking off at the canter has been solved in the most diverse manners – and this leads us to reflect that it is not a simple one.

It does appear that the famous principle of 'position and action' is insufficient to solve it, no doubt because no 'position' can *impose* the canter on the horse; some may only be *'favourable'*, and none are *'compulsive'*.

Usually, on the lead favoured by the horse – and there is always one – the central diagonal is oriented in the direction of progression and the horse consequently traverses himself more or less. However, in this position he is perfectly capable of remaining at the walk or at the trot without striking into the canter, and he can also strike off and stay at the canter in positions which are very different from that one. Furthermore, this position will vary in the case of each horse, and even in the case of one particular horse will vary considerably in degree depending on whether the horse, on a straight line, is cantering on one lead or on the other...

We must draw the conclusion that it is to the understanding of the horse that the rider must address himself and even if...he has to act more or less correctly on the *mechanics* (of the horse), he should not...be unaware of all the exceptional circumstances that can enlighten the horse to the rider's intentions.

We must not try to 'trigger' off the mechanism by infallible means, but must try to make ourselves *understood,* and let the horse *execute,* whilst we make use as best we can of what seems certain about the motion of the canter...

General Decarpentry *Academic Equitation*

Decarpentry's comments highlight three key issues: appropriate positioning of the horse; an appreciation of the mechanics of canter; and an understanding of the horse's ability to interpret signals with which he has become familiar.

With the possible exception of those who adhere completely

to the 'positioning' theory, most authorities take these three issues into consideration – although they do place their own interpretations on them. Another issue, also subject to personal interpretation, is that of educating the horse progressively in the canter aids. It is individual views on these points that lead to different opinions as to how the aids themselves are best applied. Decarpentry, who aimed to school horses to the highest level, and always had movements such as tempi changes in mind, took the view that straightness in canter was paramount:

In the case of academic equitation, the longitudinal straightness of the horse's position is of capital importance, because only this makes the changes of lead 'a tempo' possible.

We must therefore avoid all methods which cause the traversing of the horse, and adopt the one which best serves his straight position.   General Decarpentry *Academic Equitation*

Decarpentry's view of the 'capital importance' of longitudinal straightness is shared by the modern author Paul Belasik, who writes:

As soon as I began to teach horses flying changes it became very apparent why it was so necessary to teach the horse straight strike-offs in the beginning, making sure as a rider to use both legs to execute canter departures. I quickly saw how, by using one leg strongly, be it outside behind the girth or inside on the girth, I could unconsciously develop a slight swing in the horse's body, away from the stronger leg at the moment of the strike-off. In the flying change, and even more so in the multiple flying changes, the horse could sway from side to side, and any time the horse deviates sideways it will automatically be less forward, and obviously less straight.

Paul Belasik *Riding Towards the Light*

However, while Belasik seeks to resolve the problem of sideways deviation by applying equal pressure from both legs, Decarpentry's solution was different. He contended that deviation of the hindquarters was usually to the inside and that, whilst the use of the rider's outside leg behind the girth would indeed start what he called 'the evolution of the canter', it was likely to provoke or increase such deviation. For this reason he prescribed the use of interior lateral aids.

To strike off on the right lead, it will obviously be the right leg (of the rider) which will least drive the right hind to the right, and the right rein will be the most effective in preventing any turning out [of the haunches] in this direction.

The strike off obtained with 'direct leg and hand', as prescribed by Baucher in his last manner, is thus the one most suited to the demands of academic equitation.

General Decarpentry Academic Equitation

Having described the mechanical theory behind his choice of aids, Decarpentry reverts to the issues of positioning and the horse's understanding:

While trying to produce the *mechanical effects* which may produce the canter, the trainer must first of all attempt to place the horse in a whole set of extraneous circumstances which help to provoke a strike off on the lead selected and…*progressively substitute* indications still unknown to the horse to the indications which he already understands.

General Decarpentry Academic Equitation

This extract seems to suggest that the author viewed all canter aids ultimately as signals that the horse had to learn to interpret. Indeed, Decarpentry's basic method of teaching the horse to learn his canter signal entailed using the voice command to canter (preferably on the lunge – where the horse would be most familiar with it), in conjunction with the aids, gradually relinquishing the former.

Another aspect of Decarpentry's approach was that he preferred to teach the transition to canter from walk first:

We should always try to start from the walk to *begin with*, and only *later* on from the trot, particularly with horses bred from trotting stock. The ultimate transition from the canter to the canter, i.e. the flying change of lead, is always much more difficult to obtain if the horse has started with the transition to the canter from the trot, and often assumes a faulty form, consisting in a kind of intermediate trotting stride which makes the changes 'a tempo' impossible later on.

General Decarpentry *Academic Equitation*

In addition to re-affirming his long-term objective, this extract perhaps serves to place Decarpentry's work in historical and geographical context. There was a great tradition of trotting in France – where trotting races were a major equestrian sport – and it is easy to imagine that horses from trotting bloodlines would, both by temperament and conformation, pose particular problems in their education in canter.

It appears, however, that introducing canter initially from walk is not the approach favoured by most authorities: the general concerns at this stage being ease and the establishment of the basic gait, rather than the long-term objective of tempi changes. This approach is typified by Alois Podhajsky...

To start with the rider will ask the horse to strike off from a trot, which will be easier for him, and he must make use of the corners or the large circle which will put the horse in the right position to select the correct leg...The corner into the short side of the school is the best place to make the first attempt because if it does not succeed, it can immediately be tried again at the next corner.

Alois Podhajsky *The Complete Training of Horse and Rider*

...and Richard Wätjen:

When the horse has willingly learned to strike off from the trot into a canter, it can be practised from the walk, but it must be well on the bit beforehand. Here, also, the rider should be satisfied with a few exercises and a short period.

Richard Wätjen *Dressage Riding*

While Erik Herbermann writes:

One should not strike-off to the canter from the walk until well into the second year of training; the horse should be well established in walk 'on the aids'.

Erik Herbermann *Dressage Formula*

And Gustav Steinbrecht makes this observation of the horse's natural preferences:

If we now turn to the natural development of the canter, we should note initially that the horse, in freedom, almost always changes into the canter from the trot although it is very well equipped by nature to start cantering from the walk or even from the halt. Gustav Steinbrecht *The Gymnasium of the Horse*

One author who shows some sympathy with Decarpentry on this issue is Henry Wynmalen. Although Wynmalen did practice canter from trot, he acknowledged that, as schooling progressed, disadvantages could arise:

In ordinary riding, it is often customary to start at the canter from the trot. In dressage riding it is advisable not to do so. The disadvantage is two-fold.

If the horse becomes accustomed to starting at the canter from the trot, it may be very difficult to achieve a good extended trot. It is much easier for the horse, and more natural, to canter when sent on faster than to trot out...

It is also true that the rider who starts his horse from a walk has more time to place the horse and to study...the niceties of the aids. Both rider and horse will feel more finely that way and will learn more.

The practice of these starts, on either leg, is an essential preparation for the changes of leg.

Henry Wynmalen *Dressage A Study of the Finer Points of Riding*

Wynmalen also has much in common with Decarpentry in his analysis of the inherent crookedness of canter, and in his progressive refinement of the canter aids:

There is no general agreement amongst authorities as to the precise system of aids most suitable to obtain a strike-off at canter. The question is somewhat complex.

By nature, the horse does not carry himself straight at the canter. He moves somewhat sideways. When cantering with the off-fore leading, he will flex his head slightly to the right and will carry his quarters somewhat markedly to the right also. This deviation from the straight appears to be common to all four-footed animals when cantering; it is particularly noticeable in dogs.

The system most generally recommended is that of the diagonal aids. This means that, to obtain a canter with the off-fore leading, we use the right rein to obtain a flexion to the right and the left leg to activate the near-hind leg which must initiate the strike-off. It will be understood that the action of the rider's left leg must have the secondary effect of pushing the horse's quarters slightly to the right.

In other words, these diagonal aids have the effect of placing the horse in a position which conforms to the natural form of the canter; it is easy and natural for the horse to assume the canter from that position. In that respect these diagonal aids are logical and fluent and, in my opinion, we cannot do without their use in schooling our horses.

But there are inconveniences. It is impossible to obtain a perfectly straight start, or for that matter a perfectly straight canter, by the unmitigated use of the aids as described. The ancient masters were quite unconcerned about cantering somewhat sideways; in fact they delighted so much in cantering on two tracks that they were going sideways most of the time anyway.

But, and this is the quintessence of the matter, they did not practise the changes of leg! And, to obtain satisfactory changes of leg, especially at short intervals, the horse must canter straight.

So, it is a basic requirement of the modern school that the horse shall start straight at the canter.

Let us then examine these aids a little more closely.

The use of the right rein causes a flexion to the right. But it also acts to some extent as rein of opposition to the haunches, tending to prevent the quarters from swinging to the right. However, that effect is only light and insufficient to offset the effect of the left leg, particularly if that left leg is applied behind the girth.

Accordingly, when our horse is sufficiently advanced in his ordinary training to warrant us thinking about straightening his canter, we have to incorporate some gradual modifications and refinements in these aids.

Since the horse is so very observant, there is...no great difficulty, provided we proceed step by step.

In the first place then we concentrate, if we have not already done so...on using the rein-aid as a preliminary warning signal only. To obtain that effect we introduce a slight time-lapse between the moment when we touch a rein and the moment of applying our leg. Incidentally, this time-lapse is in truth always essential because it would be difficult, without it, to avoid a restraining effect of the rein at the very moment when the horse strikes off at the canter...

However, our main object now is to agree with the horse that a slight touch on the right rein means that an order to strike-off with the off-fore leading is about to follow; and similarly, of course, a touch on the left rein precedes a left canter.

Once that convention has been established, there is no longer any need to apply the directing leg anywhere but quite close to the girth. For instance, to obtain a strike-off on the off-fore, we touch the right rein, followed by a touch of the left leg close to the girth.

That is already some progress, though still insufficient to ensure straightness.

Accordingly, we progress further by using both legs close behind the girth, exactly as we would do for moving off in trot. Risk of confusion does not arise, since the canter, and the particular leg to canter on, have already been determined by the preceding rein-signal.

Continuing in this manner, we will soon be able to use one or other of our legs more predominately...again without the risk of confusion, thanks to our rein signal. This implies that we can now use both legs, or any one of them as occasion may demand, for the dual purpose of obtaining the strike-off and/or for dressing the quarters straight before, during and after the take-off.

In other words, we are now so far that we can use diagonal or lateral aids or a mixture of both, according to circumstances, without fear of being misunderstood...

Henry Wynmalen *Dressage A Study of the Finer Points of Riding*

It is interesting to compare these points with an extract from Wynmalen's earlier work, *Equitation*. Whereas, in the above, Wynmalen was describing the progressive refinement of the canter aids, at this point in *Equitation* he was more concerned with the introduction of canter.

To strike off, with the off-fore leading, the aids are: left or outside leg 'closed' behind the girth (with the right or inside leg 'closed' on the girth to press the horse forward and into his bridle) and a 'feel' on the right rein, a true diagonal aid once more. The rider's left leg drives the near-hind under for the take-off stride...and the feel on the right rein produces a flexion to the right.

Though these indications will suffice for the well-schooled horse, I will have to accentuate them to some extent in the beginning, in order to teach my horse the meaning of them. This accentuation I obtain by pulling my right rein in an upward direction, so as to raise the horse's head and lighten his forehand, while I simultaneously carry both hands to the left, thus bringing the weight on the near fore and lightening the off-fore.

The horse placed in this position on entering a corner to the right is almost certain to strike off correctly.

Henry Wynmalen *Equitation*

This description is followed by the observation that:

Although no one, in equitation, would use any other than diagonal aids for the canter, I ought to acknowledge that a large number of riders...in England still continue to use lateral aids.

Henry Wynmalen *Equitation*

The first point of note here is that, at the time of writing *Equitation*, Wynmalen appears to have had a less expansive view of the canter aids than he was to adopt later. The second point is that the 'lateral aids' he proceeds to attack are not the interior laterals aids, as advocated by Baucher, Decarpentry and others, but exterior lateral aids, intended to impose a canter lead through loss of balance. Aids of this sort are referred to, and dismissed, by Wilhelm Müseler:

Cantering on is taught in different ways. One can make a horse canter on either by the whip or by the voice or even by a click of the tongue. It is often said that the horse should be flexed towards the outside so as to give him more freedom in the shoulders (in which case the flexion would be something like an S). Again, riders are often recommended to canter on only by means of the outer leg. All such advice is misleading...

Wilhelm Müseler *Riding Logic*

Wynmalen has this to say of them:

These aids are called 'lateral' because the rider uses leg and rein-aid to one side of the horse only; in other words, to obtain a strike-off with the off-fore leading, such riders use the left leg and the left rein, whereas the adherents of diagonal aids would use the left leg and the right rein.

Let it be recognised first of all, that as all aids are but a conventional language between rider and horse, it is just as easy to teach a horse to respond to one set of indications as to another.

In fact, it is undoubtedly easier and requires less horsemanship to obtain the required lead from an unschooled or poorly schooled horse with lateral than with diagonal aids. [The author then quotes from a chapter entitled 'Advanced Horsemanship' in an old cavalryman's manual.]

'To strike a horse off on the near-fore the horse's head is turned slightly to the right, the pace slightly increased, and the right leg applied stronger than the left. If the horse will obey the leg as he should...this will have the effect of slightly over-balancing him to the left. He very naturally puts out the near-fore and near-hind to save himself.'

In other words, the horse cannot help himself, and the system is therefore very easy, but I fail to see anything advanced in it.

For in horsemanship, as I understand it, our endeavour should be to balance our horse to the movement that we require, and not to obtain such movement by...throwing him off balance!

But the fact remains that these lateral aids are easy, and are therefore suitable for such riders...as lack the necessary knowledge to position their horses...They are also suitable for those riders who want to make their horses canter before the horse [is] capable of being positioned.

This latter contention is borne out by the fact that at the Equitation School, Weedon [the old British Cavalry School], green horses were taught to canter by means of lateral aids, but that diagonal aids were resorted to as soon as the horse's progress permitted it.

And the reason for this change-over from one system to another (and in my opinion this...dual system is neither logical nor consequent) is the very obvious one, that lateral aids for the canter are entirely and totally unsuited for any of the more advanced work, such as changes of leg...

For the exhibitions of this exercise by the lateral-aid brigade are not changes at all, as understood in equitation, smooth, balanced and straight; their horses, thrown off their balance by the often violent contortions of their riders, are merely changing to save themselves from falling.

No, in equitation our aim is to place our horse always in the correct balance for the movement that we require, which we call 'positioning'. Now when a horse canters with the off-fore leading he must be flexed in the direction of that movement, in other words he must be 'right-positioned'. And by applying our diagonal aids we obtain this correct position from the very beginning, in fact from before the movement actually begins!

Henry Wynmalen *Equitation*

At this point, it is perhaps fair to point out that not everyone associated with Weedon subscribed to the methods mentioned by Wynmalen. Major-General Geoffrey Brooke, from the stable of genuinely all-round horsemen, had a long involvement with dressage, showjumping, hunting and racing. As a Lt. Colonel he was, in the 1920s, Chief Instructor to the British Cavalry School. In his book *Horsemanship Dressage & Show-Jumping*, first published in 1929, Brooke describes aids for the transition to canter right which are very similar to the early diagonal aids described by Wynmalen:

Collect the horse, carry the right hand towards the withers to the left with an increased feeling of the right rein, the muzzle being inclined slightly to the right: close both legs, the left leg the stronger, and press the horse up to a canter. The rider should not lean over to the right.

Geoffrey Brooke *Horsemanship Dressage & Show-Jumping*

It is also interesting to note that, while he did not advocate provoking canter by unbalancing the horse, the German Master,

Gustav Steinbrecht, observed differences between the transitions to canter of the young horse and his more highly trained counterpart, with different aids being seen effectively as a *consequence* of this:

The transition [of the novice horse] generally takes place in that the trotting horse moves one foreleg forward more quickly and farther out than the diagonally opposite hind leg in order to support the weight that is being moved forward. The hind leg is thus prevented from stepping forward and transfers the load that much faster to the other two diagonal legs of which the inside hind leg by nature steps that much more forward the more the outside hind leg remains behind. In this way there first results an impure trot, a three-beat movement, from which the horse then falls into the canter. This observation indicates that, if we want to canter a young horse during its first training phases, before we have collected the trot, we only have available the development of the canter that the horse uses naturally. Our aids will therefore reside in restraining the outside shoulder with the outside rein, thus holding back the outside foreleg to give more freedom to the inside shoulder and its foreleg, while our inside leg urges the inside hind leg to step further forward. In addition, we relieve the inner side by putting more of our weight on the outside seat bone.

Gustav Steinbrecht *The Gymnasium of the Horse*

In this context, Steinbrecht seems to be describing a reversed form of diagonal aids. He continues:

In this connection it should be pointed out right away that the trained horse that starts cantering from the collected trot performs a different transition. Here, after the inside diagonal has been put down, the outside hind leg is caused to step off early by the rider's leg on the same side. Then the inside foreleg first pushes the horse's body into the freely suspended phase and the previously put down outside hind leg reaches the ground first, earlier than the two simultaneously tracking legs of the other diagonal.   Gustav Steinbrecht *The Gymnasium of the Horse*

Indicating that, at this more advanced stage, the rider's outside leg is now being used to instigate the transition.

André Jousseaume was a graduate of Saumur and a contemporary of General Decarpentry. His approach to canter shows some similarities to, and some differences from, that of Decarpentry. An advocate of limited early canter work for its suppling value, Jousseaume's description of the initial canter aids has a resonance of Steinbrecht's reference to the young horse 'falling' into canter.

To obtain a depart on the inside leg, make the horse trot on a large circle, the rider posting on the inside diagonal (inside foreleg and outside hindleg). Then extend the trot and take advantage of the end of the riding school to push the trot to its limit, so that the horse falls into the canter at the turn, which will help him to strike off on the correct lead. At the same time, use the rein of indirect opposition in front of the withers...This is the canter depart by 'loss of equilibrium' which should...be used during early training.

André Jousseaume *Progressive Dressage*

While Henry Wynmalen's view of this method might have been open to question, it is somewhat different from the laterally unbalancing exterior aids which Wynmalen so disliked. However, Jousseaume, like Wynmalen and Decarpentry, used a progressive method of introducing canter, and goes on talk of establishing the canter departs by the 'taking of equilibrium':

Steps to follow:
1. Canter depart from sitting trot on the circle.
2. Canter depart from sitting trot on the straight line.
3. Canter depart from the walk on the circle.
4. Canter depart from the walk on the straight line.

André Jousseaume *Progressive Dressage*

It is noticeable that the progression of these steps does not comply with Decarpentry's view of starting with canter from walk, but there is a marked similarity of views regarding the progressive establishment of a 'convention of aids':

When commencing, the aids used are not the same as those which will be used at the end of training. There is a conventional language to be established between the rider and the horse.

The actions must be excessively clear and precise at the beginning, so that the horse may easily understand. Later, the goal will be to obtain a canter depart (to the right, for example), solely by a light indication of the right rein and the action of the inside leg (right leg).

However, at first, the aids to be used are as follows:

Depart on the right lead.

(a) Right rein to demand the bend to the right, and seat to the left to unweight the right lateral.

(b) Light tension on the left rein to limit curving of the neck.

(c) Preponderant left leg acting as an isolated leg.

(d) Right leg. The action of the left leg results in displacement of the haunches toward the right. The right leg intervenes at the girth (without discontinuing left leg action) at the instant when this displacement is going to take place to transform it into a forward movement at the canter.

(e) At the same time, slightly close the fingers on the right rein while raising the right hand a little. This action may give the rider the impression from which comes the expression 'to pick up the forehand'. However, the rider cannot have the pretension of picking up the forehand. Actually, this action of the hand, which must be light and discreet, is only an indication for the horse, but indication enough to create the reflex due to the fact that the horse is placed in a position and equilibrium which are favourable to the canter depart.

(f) Yielding of both hands at the instant of the depart. The horse should not come up against the hand. At this stage of training, if correctly demanded; the canter depart should pose no difficulties...

...As the training progresses and when the horse no longer hesitates, the outside leg...will become less and less preponderant up to the point of ...[obtaining] the depart with both legs equal and a simple action of the right rein.

Of the transition at a more advanced stage, Jousseaume writes:

Departs should now be demanded with equal legs and a light indication of the hand on the side of the bend. They may also be demanded by a preponderant action of the inside leg...but the other leg must always be ready to act in case the horse hesitates in taking the desired lead.

In fact, the canter depart with the inside leg now becomes a question of reflex, because the preponderance of the inside leg has only a conventional value. The...horse can avoid its action each time he wishes. Thus, the outside leg must, at each instant, nip in the bud any tendency toward disobedience by forming a wall on its side.

Some masters say that perfectly straight departs are obtained with the inside leg. There is no doubt about this, but the same result can also be obtained with equal action of both legs and, in my opinion, this procedure has the advantage of superior impulsion with a more energetic thrust of the hindleg which begins the first stride.

However, with the goal of refining the horse's reflexes and making him more and more attentive, it is a good idea to work on the canter depart with the inside leg.

André Jousseaume *Progressive Dressage*

In other words, he shares the opinion of Decarpentry and Wynmalen that interior lateral aids are the ideal in principle. However, be agrees with Wynmalen that, in practice, appropriate use of the rider's outside leg may be necessary – and makes the point that, in terms of increasing impulsion, it may always remain desirable.

Another authority who believed in a progressive approach to canter was Waldemar Seunig. He was a great advocate of allowing the young horse simply to get used to cantering under the rider's weight in the open, whilst developing his strength and balance in the school at trot. In this context, his emphasis on introducing the school transitions to canter from 'a moderated working trot' is noteworthy…

If we tried a gallop depart from a fast trot, it would be harder for the horse because the legs required for the initial thrust would not be immediately available, owing to the longer phase of suspension, especially as they are further apart at an extended rate.

Waldemar Seunig *Horsemanship*

…and helps explain why the initial method described by Jousseaume relies on the horse 'falling' into canter.

Seunig's introduction of transitions to canter in the school involved the use of spiralling circles or shoulder-fore to aid 'positioning':

The horse must be able to carry himself in a moderated working trot and must be able to obey the sideways driving aids in the decreasing and increasing spiral circles. Whereas the horse in the open has so far selected his own canter lead, he must now learn in the riding school to take the correct canter lead. The circle size is decreased at a slightly shortened working trot and then increased. Upon re-establishing the original dimension of the circle, preferably on the open side just before reaching the wall, the outside leg supported by the…outside rein establishes contact with the convex side of the horse and limits the sideways movement. At the same time, the inside leg drives to the fore. Whip is on the outside shoulder and the familiar voice aid reinforces the request for canter. Inside hand at first gives a little, but nevertheless a slight bending at the poll to the inside must be maintained.

With a relaxed acceptance to the forward driving aids, the horse will now naturally and with certainty find the correct canter lead.

Equally recommended is a second way of breaking into canter, which is based on the same principle as the first…However, this method assumes that the horse through lateral flexion work has achieved a higher degree of suppleness and the ability to become collected… We take the horse which is going in the shortened working trot on the circle in the shoulder-fore position and give, after a few strides, the above-mentioned aids to canter. At the same time, we reposition the forehand which has moved a little to the inside, and it now returns to its former position on the circle. The slight swing to the outside by the leading shoulder requires a considerable degree of attention and sensitivity on the part of the horse.

Waldemar Seunig *The Essence of Horsemanship*

Seunig had referred to the value of shoulder-in flexion in his earlier book, *Horsemanship:*

We mention the gallop depart from the preceding shoulder-in flexion...because it is the best and most dependable way of correcting the fault of turning the hindquarters towards the inside in order to escape the even loading of all four legs. This is a fault that creeps in unnoticed but is nonetheless very serious...

...and had made interesting points about the natural aspect of 'position' and the balancing function of the horse's outside hind:

...the 'position' should be adopted at the gallop if only because it is spontaneously offered to the rider as something quite natural...by every horse moving without constraint. It must be supervised by the inside leg only to the extent of seeing that the loading of the horse's four legs remains even and that the inside hind leg keeps to the line from the inside ear to the inside shoulder...when moving on a single track. A horse that is moving correctly at a gallop requires this natural flexion of the ribs for reasons of locomotion alone. It must be able to place the outside hind foot, which at times lifts the entire load and sustains it upon alighting after the suspension phase, vertically beneath the line passing through the centre of that load, thus supporting the latter under mechanical conditions that are best for thrust and load support.

Thus the...'sense of balance', possessed by every living thing, causes the horse not to track with its outside hind foot exactly in the trace of the corresponding front foot.

Waldemar Seunig *Horsemanship*

In *The Essence of Horsemanship* he went on to say of his methods that:

Young horses who have been schooled from the very beginning to break into the canter from a widening of the circle or from the shoulder-fore position will, with the application of correct aids, never even dream of breaking into the wrong lead by putting the hindquarters to the inside, a bad mistake, which, once rooted, is almost impossible to erase and which will hinder further progress. In order to prevent this error from sneaking in, we avoid even 'for the sake of learning' the beloved transition to the canter out of the corner.

Waldemar Seunig *The Essence of Horsemanship*

It seems likely that Seunig's reservations about using the corner for transitions may have developed through experience. In the earlier *Horsemanship,* whilst giving precedence to the use of spiralling circles, he does mention using the corner – albeit with a caveat against provoking anticipation:

If lateral responsiveness is not sufficiently positive to enable the horse to develop the gallop from…enlargement of the circle, we can also exercise the…depart from the corner preceding a long wall – again from the shortened working trot. Here, too, the controls will have the desired effect; brief pressure with both legs, greater pressure being exercised by the inside leg, with an increased shift of the rider's load to the inner seat bone as is automatically effected by the seat in the turn, and the sustaining action of the outside rein. The rider should not use the same corner over and over again, for this will make lively horses grow restless…they will become refractory and anticipate the controls.

Waldemar Seunig *Horsemanship*

Of the aids themselves, Seunig says:

To commence the canter the described aids should become

increasingly hints only. Ultimately only the slightest indication by the inside rein and a stretching of the inside leg should be necessary. The more quietly the schooling proceeds, the quieter and softer the ensuing canter will be. At the very moment the horse picks himself up for the first canter stride, the rider's hand gives slightly and his lower back and legs direct the flow of the movement. During the canter, the rider follows the forward movement well with a deep seat.

Waldemar Seunig *The Essence of Horsemanship*

So it seems that, like Decarpentry, Seunig worked towards producing the canter from interior lateral aids.

Wilhelm Müseler was another authority who emphasised the value of positioning prior to canter. While Müseler was a great advocate of seat and back aids, he describes here an interplay of aids for both the positioning and the transition:

The aid for cantering does not begin from the normal or straight seat but from the seat which the rider must assume if he wishes to flex his horse either towards the left or towards the right. Consequently, the inner hip is pushed forward, the inner leg has close contact at the girth, the outer one being approximately a hand behind the girth. If the rider now quietly urges his horse forward with his back and both legs, at the same time giving the reins, the horse will trot on in position left or position right.

In order to put the horse into a canter and not into a trot, the...foot-fall must be altered. This is mainly effected by a very energetic forward push of the inner pelvic bone and by the unilateral bracing of the back-muscles. In this connection both legs press the horse forward (the inner at the girth, the outer one half a hand behind the girth). Both reins must give equally in order to let the movement come out forward...

Wilhelm Müseler *Riding Logic*

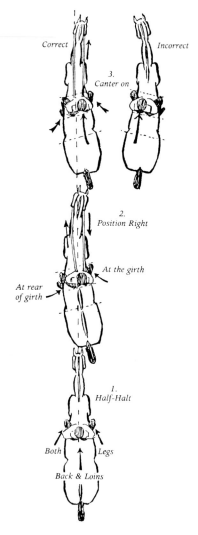

Correct   Incorrect

3.
Canter on

2.
Position Right

At the girth

At rear
of girth

1.
Half-Halt

Both   Legs

Back & Loins

49. Canter on the right.

Illustrations of position right from Müseler's Riding Logic.

This interplay of aids is emphasised by most Masters, albeit in slightly different terms and with differing emphasis upon their precise roles. Here are the canter aids as described by two Directors of the Spanish Riding School...

The leg aids for canter are also based on physical laws. The restraining outside leg (together with the outside rein) holds the outside shoulder of the horse for a moment, thus freeing the inside shoulder. The inside leg, just behind the girth, encourages the advance of the inside shoulder. It is in this manner that the horse is aided to start the canter. In theory, each spring of the canter has to be determined by the same aids; in practice however the leg aids need only be sufficiently energetic to be felt by the horse if the rider feels that the 'springs of the motor' are slackening; a good rider will act in good time to prevent a breaking of the canter.   Kurt Albrecht *Principles of Dressage*

The outside leg placed passively behind the girth gives the signal for the canter and prevents the horse from carrying his hindquarters to the outside, while the inside leg, pushing forward on the girth, makes the horse strike off. At the same time the rider must sit a little more firmly on his inside seat bone. With the transition to the canter the rider must be careful not to allow his inside leg to slide forward as so often happens, thus diminishing the value of the aid in this pace. The inside rein must place the horse in the right position and, with the support of the inside leg, prevent the hindquarters from falling in, which would cause a crooked strike-off, a serious fault not to be allowed even with the young horse.

Alois Podhajsky   *The Complete Training of Horse and Rider*

...by Richard Wätjen, a Spanish Riding School pupil who went on to become an Olympic trainer:

The inside leg of the rider should act on the girth, the outside leg slightly behind it; the position is maintained by the outside rein. When striking off a young horse into canter, the animal should be well on the bit before applying the driving aids. Half halts prevent the horse from running on and pressing to the inside, without influencing the proper head and neck position. At the same moment the leg aids must be given correctly and with sufficient strength…When it is on the proper leg, the rider has to support and maintain the canter with both legs but mainly with the *inside* one. An exaggerated seat, weight aids and support with the rein should be avoided, as these would restrain the impulsion and impair the sensitiveness of a young horse.

Richard Wätjen *Dressage Riding*

…and by a Dressage World Champion:

How does one canter on? A big circle is ridden in working trot and a half-halt asked for at the wall side of the circle. The rider then shifts his weight to the inside by pushing the inside hip forwards and putting more weight on the inside stirrup. The rider then puts the outside leg behind the girth and takes a light contact with the inside rein. He then asks for the canter by pushing the inside seatbone forwards in connection with a tightening of the back muscles and pressure from both legs (the inside on the girth, the outside behind the girth) and an easing of the inside rein.   Reiner Klimke *Basic Training of the Young Horse*

Here, talking about introductory canter aids for the young horse, Klimke is breaking them down into segments. In his book *Dressage Formula*, Erik Herbermann also analyses the component elements of the canter aids, and summarises the progression to canter thus:

- Horse clearly bent around the inside leg; soft and accepting on *both* reins.
- Rider's inside leg in the normal position near the girth; outside leg well back.
- Rider sits relaxed, with a nicely stretched body position, and the inside seat bone slightly forward.
- The *outside* leg (passively applied) says, 'AND', then the *inside* seat bone, applying greater weight and forward-urging pressure, says, 'can-TER'! If the horse doesn't react crisply to the inside seat bone alone, the inside leg may give an *active* nudge at the same time, and even this may be further reinforced with a tap from the stick, if necessary. The outside leg gives the same pressure but is held passively. A half-halt is given just before the aid to canter-on. This balances the horse and frees it from the hand. We must clearly lighten the hands, especially the inside rein, at the canter strike-off.
- To maintain the canter, the aid to 'canter-on' is repeated at each stride, more or less. This might be just 'the subtlest of hints' from the inside seat bone only, or a fairly loud aid with the 'full orchestra', as the moment requires.

Erik Herbermann   Dressage Formula

Pointers for Early Canter

One theme that is common to the writing of many Masters is patience; the horse is allowed time to develop both his understanding and his physical ability. Another theme is the precedence given to key principles. Here, Richard Wätjen stresses the early precedence of 'forward and straight' over matters such as outline:

In the elementary stages little attention should be paid to the head and neck position. Only when it strikes off *easily and without any effort* should the rider gradually endeavour to obtain a proper head and neck position. In all paces the horse should move *freely forward and with impulsion*...

...Even in the elementary stages the rider must train his horse to canter straight forward *on one track*. It must always have enough freedom to move freely and naturally forward. The rider's inside leg must remain firmly on the girth and continually *support the horse's inside hindleg*.

Richard Wätjen *Dressage Riding*

While Alois Podhajsky emphasises the need for calm progression:

If the horse when asked for canter instead dashes off into a fast trot, he must not be allowed to strike off from this pace; he must be slowed down and calmed before being asked again.

Alois Podhajsky The Complete Training of Horse and Rider

There is a marked difference between running in trot in response to the canter aids and the extreme reaction described here by Waldemar Seunig. Seunig's prescribed remedy makes the point that the rider should always be thinking 'forwards'.

The transition to gallop...may not proceed so smoothly with all horses; some will immediately grow excited and want to bolt. One should not hold such horses back by restraining rein controls; this would merely increase their excitement. They would fight the rider's hands and learn how to stiffen their hindquarters and back against the...restraining seat.

It is far better for the rider to allow his seat to go along with the horse and to have his driving controls remain in contact as if he wished to increase the rate still more. If this is done, the suggestion of compulsion will soon vanish...

Waldemar Seunig *Horsemanship*

Taking an overview of early transitions, Gustav Steinbrecht points out that skill and sympathy on the rider's part will produce far better results than impatience and force:

In the first development of the canter it is only important to practice a quiet canter depart...For this purpose, the rider must not push the horse into the canter with sudden, hard or even rough aids; instead he must use lightly touching leg aids which are skillfully supported by his voice...and whip, to repeatedly ask the horse to reach out with its inside legs. Horses that tend to rush away at the trot when they receive the driving aids must always be taken back into a restrained trot tempo before the above-described driving aids are given again.

Likewise, horses that are unable to carry themselves sufficiently in the canter because of insufficient natural self-carriage and therefore soon drop back into the trot must not be pushed back into the canter immediately with stronger aids, but instead returned to a quiet, regular trot...before another attempt can be made to make them canter.

Gustav Steinbrecht *The Gymnasium of the Horse*

A philosophy which is shared by Erik Herbermann:

Be careful not to force or surprise the horse with the canter aid, as tensions and rushing will result. With young horses it is best to strike-off to the canter from the trot, using the corner of the school to help juggle-up the correct lead. One may need to reinforce the canter aid with the stick (either at the horse's inside shoulder, or behind the rider's outside leg), until the horse becomes familiar with the signal from seat (weight aid) and leg alone...

It is a common mistake to force the horse back into the canter immediately after it has fallen from the canter into an unbalanced, rushing trot. When this happens, the rider should instead always take time to bring the horse back down quietly into a good, rhythmic, balanced and relaxed trot before striking-off into canter once again. With more advanced horses one should make the transition down to the walk before commencing the canter again; this improves the balance, suppleness and use of the back, and the engagement of the hindquarters.

Erik Herbermann *Dressage Formula*

The Rider

Whatever precise combination of aids is chosen to start and maintain the canter, the rider will have little hope of success without a good seat and a 'feel' for the movement. In his book *The Complete Training of Horse and Rider* Alois Podhajsky makes the point that:

When the rider has obtained the necessary firmness and independence of seat, especially in the increased tempo of trot, *work at the canter* may begin. This work should not be considered until the rider's seat is sufficiently firm, because the canter demands a stronger application of the aids than the other paces.

Alois Podhajsky *The Complete Training of Horse and Rider*

In *Fundamentals of Riding* Charles Harris, who studied under Podhajsky, describes the sensations and actions of the rider's seat in canter:

The rider's position at the canter is perhaps the most difficult of all the gaits to master, and carry out satisfactorily. Because of this, few have been able to teach, or describe the action of the rider's seat and body posture with accuracy and sensitivity. The sequence of seat sensations/actions/feels, varies according to the length of the canter stride, and at each complete stride...

Sequence of seat sensations at canter

1. *The immediate lowering/sinking of the seat* by slightly relaxing the seat and loins, at one and the same time, and having reached the lowest point...
2. *Floating forward of the seat,* with upright/supple body posture, with a gradual firming of the loins, but not that of the buttocks which remain soft/supple and relaxed. This immediately becomes the basis for, and part of...
3. *The gentle floating/forward upward following a 'comfortable concave arc',* as if the rider's seat was 'stitched to the saddle seat'. This completes the first stride, and without any break into No. 1 again, the immediate lowering/sinking of the seat...

These three quite separate and distinct sensations/actions/feels, are blended into one *flowing movement* – down/forward/upward – at every stride of the canter, only being slightly modified to suit the length and/or elevation of the canter stride(s).

At no point in the canter stride – or from one canter stride to the next should the weight of the rider – through the medium of the seat – ease/lift itself upward and away from the saddle...

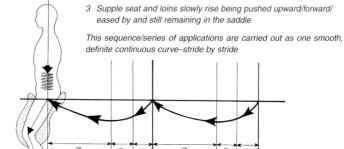

1 Thighs remain 'adhesive' on the saddle flaps during the sinking of a supple seat and loins

2 Floating forward of the supple seat (buttocks and loins) always remaining and bottoming on the saddle seat

3 Supple seat and loins slowly rise being pushed upward/forward/eased by and still remaining in the saddle

This sequence/series of applications are carried out as one smooth, definite continuous curve–stride by stride

Canter – correct seat never leaving saddle

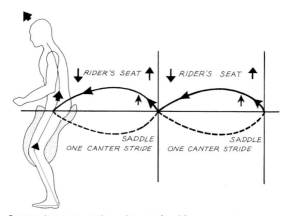

Canter – incorrect seat bouncing out of saddle

Illustrations of correct and incorrect seat at canter, from
Fundamentals of Riding *by Charles Harris.*

The pleasure of riding at the canter is its smooth/regular undulating 'swing', flowing in the saddle without any jarring or concussion whatsoever throughout the whole body

Charles Harris *Fundamentals of Riding*

The relationship between a good seat and a 'feel' for the canter is described by Henry Wynmalen:

For the sake of clarity, we have, so far, only considered the horse's tendency to deviate from a straight line...at the canter and the actions of hand and leg which are at the rider's disposal, subject to careful progressive schooling, to obviate that tendency.

It is still necessary to mention a further peculiarity of the gait which influences the rider's seat.

When a horse canters with the off-fore leading, his off-fore and his off-hind will always touch down well in front of the hoof-prints made by the near-fore and the near-hind legs, and vice versa when the near-fore is leading.

Accordingly, when cantering with the off-fore leading, the horse's right shoulder and his right hip are somewhat in advance of his left shoulder and left hip. The feel of this position is transmitted to the rider's seat by the action of the muscles which determine it. Accordingly, the sensitive rider will adjust his seat by intuition in conformity with the feel given him by the horse. This means that, when the horse is cantering to the right, the rider will assume a position in the saddle with his right seat bone slightly in advance of the left...And, just as much as the rider can feel his horse's position under the saddle, so the horse can feel the rider's position in the saddle.

In so doing, the rider assists unity of balance...More than that, this refinement of the rider's position...clearly perceived by the sensitive horse, becomes an aid by association.

Henry Wynmalen *Dressage A Study of the Finer Points of Riding*

And by Wilhelm Müseler:

A rider canters correctly if he sits in complete harmony, i.e. as the horse's movements require. All doubts can be removed by testing oneself. If you cannot feel whether your horse canters on the wrong leg, then you may rest assured that your seat is wrong…

The trained horse bends a little towards the right when leading on the off fore and to the left when leading on the near fore, and not only is the inner pair of legs in advance…but the whole of his muscles, including those of the inward bent back, work in accordance with this flexion. If the rider now endeavours to follow this movement, and stick to the saddle…he must push his inner pelvic bone and his hips forward by a unilateral bracing of the back. If he has properly learned to do that he can stick to the saddle at the canter with the same ease as at the trot.

If the rider pushes the inner side forward and the horse tries to canter on, leading on the opposite leg, the rider would no more be sitting in harmony, and could not therefore remain glued to the saddle. The rider must feel with his buttocks whether the horse is leading on the wrong leg, for the horse will try to seat him differently from the way he wishes to sit. Whereas he wants to push his right hip and right pelvic bone forward, the horse pushes his left hip and left pelvic bone forward. Obviously a kind of rotating movement results, and this he must feel under his buttocks, because it prevents him from remaining glued to the saddle. When the rider has been taught to pay attention to this the feel for it will soon develop.

Wilhelm Müseler *Riding Logic*

While Ulrik Schramm emphasises the value of feel and timing in the application of the rider's leg:

At the canter, the driving aids must coincide with the moment at which the inside hind is lifted and stifle and hock flex to swing it forwards...What matters to the rider is the promotion of the vigorous forward swing of the inside hind which must advance sufficiently to balance the combined weight of horse and rider. We must learn to feel the moment at which our predominantly driving inside leg can produce this effect; again, we are given the clue by the horse, because it will arch its rib cage towards the side of the swinging inside hindlimb; at the same time, the horse will feel as if it were lifting up its forehand.

Ulrik Schramm The Undisciplined Horse

Developing the Working Canter

The first point that the Masters make about developing the canter is this is not achieved by protracted periods of work...

To strengthen the horse in the canter, the canter exercises should initially be very short and should only gradually be extended for longer periods...after the horse's fitness state increases...   Gustav Steinbrecht *The Gymnasium of the Horse*

It would be wrong to canter for any length of time...To canter for long does not improve the canter stride. The horse gets tired and loses its 'schwung' and the hind quarters are dragged along.
    Reiner Klimke *Basic Training of the Young Horse*

...but by work of the right kind:

Experience shows that the best way to develop the canter is by frequent transitions on the circle between trot to canter.
    Reiner Klimke *Basic Training of the Young Horse*

Transitions and circle work are also recommended by Nuno Oliveira:

A horse is not taught balance at the canter by cantering for a long time, but rather by doing frequent strike offs from the walk and from the halt.

Working the horse in circles is one of the most successful ways to give him suppleness, regularity and grace in his canter. The circular movement forces him to try to gain good balance, activates him, and places the hind legs under the mass.

Nuno Oliveira *Notes and Reminiscences of a Portuguese Rider*

Klimke's reference to the quality of movement is echoed by Erik Herbermann:

By its very nature – a series of jumps – canter is the most impulsive gait. Nonetheless, special care must be focused on maintaining a true forward urge and balance.

Erik Herbermann *Dressage Formula*

This emphasis on natural, forward movement – especially in the formative stage of canter – is repeated by Seunig:

The natural leap displayed by the horse the first time it gallops in the riding hall should be retained for the moment, being modified…only after some days have passed. Driving or restraining controls develop an even rate, the working gallop…

The way in which these 'driving and restraining controls' are introduced – especially in the context of shortening and balancing the natural canter – can make or mar the gait. In this connection, Seunig makes a point which has significance far beyond the development of canter:

The most rapid positive progress is made by the rider who is so psychologically balanced that he is prepared for a long period of training, governed solely by the progress made by the horse.

Regarding the actual process of shortening the working gait, he writes:

Though the first collection at the trot is best achieved...by gathering it from a smooth and spirited middle trot, the gait of the working gallop is shortened by means of frequent gallop departs from walk. The transition from the walk to the gallop is made...when the horse's contact with the bit at the walk has become a positive one with slightly shortened reins. The horse, which is already familiar with gallop departs, will respond readily to the controls...especially if it is allowed to take a few trotting strides at the beginning and if the gallop departs are taken from the corner or the volte for the first few times.

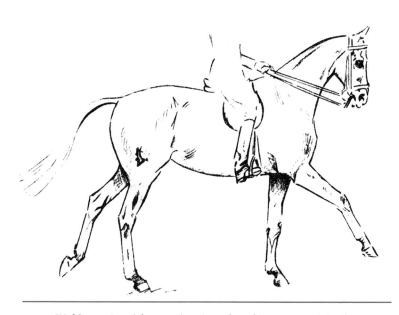

Waldemar Seunig's own drawing of working canter right, from
The Essence of Horsemanship.

Adding:

The natural limit to shortening the gait of the working gallop is preservation of the right gait and contact with the bit. Here are infallible signs that too much has been asked of the horse for the time being:

(1) Its movements lose their lively springiness and become flat and dragging.

(2) The rider no longer is pulled forward in the saddle by the horse's elastically pulsating back. As a result, his inside leg no longer clings without effort to its place alongside the horse's ribs, which fall inward somewhat.

(3) The feel becomes dead or uneven in the rider's hands and jerky in his seat.   Waldemar Seunig *Horsemanship*

Seunig's distinction between the methods of shortening the working gait at trot and canter strikes a chord with these words of Steinbrecht, which include a succinct summary of the aims of working canter:

...at the canter, the activity of the limbs differs significantly from that in the walk and trot, and this circumstance must be considered in the development and perfection of the canter to prevent disadvantageous consequences from resulting...To initially explain what it is that we desire when working the horse at canter: it is nothing other than to enable the horse, by way of gradually increasing gymnastic exercises, to move with ease in this gait...This goal, the self-carriage, can be realised at the canter, just like at the trot, only by getting the horse to relax and setting it straight through bending work, thus creating the basis on which self-carriage is founded, namely the rider in balance with the horse.   Gustav Steinbrecht *The Gymnasium of the Horse*

Erik Herbermann on Atlantis. Shortened working canter right.
From Herbermann's Dressage Formula.

A further view of the qualities desired in working canter is given by Lt. Col. d'Endrödy, in this description of the gait as required in a three-day event dressage test:

The movements as a whole must be light and cadenced on account of the swinging action of the back. The strides should be free, with definite ground-covering character. The horse's bearing must show a moderately arched head- and neck-carriage and it should go softly into the bridle.

Lt. Col. A.L. d'Endrödy *Give Your Horse A Chance*

Discussing the criteria required by judges of canter work at Elementary level, Kurt Albrecht writes:

The horse must have learned to execute the transition to canter in both directions upon the indication of the aids and exactly at the point specified. This proves that it has been taught to understand the aids and to obey them instantly. Moreover, the joints of the hindquarters, and particularly the hocks, must have become resilient enough to allow the horse to spring immediately into canter on command since the outside hind alone has to support the mass and thrust it forward for the first spring. To this end the collecting aids (i.e. half-halts) have to permeate the entire mass to reach the hocks and again this is possible only if the head and neck position are correct.

If the horse still needs momentum to get into canter, and speed to continue cantering, it shows that it has not yet got the strength to preserve horizontal equilibrium. The rein effects are then only hand actions without the collecting effect of correct half-halts. It also shows that the rider does not know how to use his legs to control the hindquarters...

A rider who sits up with supple loins and keeps his lower legs in constant contact with the horse's sides helps the horse to

The *Canter* will develop more easily from a
well-established trot, and just as the
trot is the basis of schooling on
the ground, the canter is the
basis of movements
above the ground.

Engraving from Johann Ridinger, reproduced in Albrecht's
A Dressage Judge's Handbook.

canter straight by setting both hind legs under its body.

Kurt Albrecht *A Dressage Judge's Handbook*

While, also on the topics of speed and equilibrium, Nuno Oliveira writes:

During canter departs the horse should elevate his forehand rather than throwing himself forward...

Adding that:

In order to have a nice rocking type of canter instead of a forced flattened out one, the horse must be straight, so try not to over-bend him, avoiding the use of the inside rein as much as possible, and conserve the cadence by placing the horse's shoulders properly. In this pace, the outside rein serves to set the horse back on his haunches while the inside rein elongates and lowers the neck.

Nuno Oliveira *Notes and Reminiscences of a Portuguese Rider*

Faults in the
Working Canter

With canter being such a complex gait, it is not surprising that the potential exists for many faults. Perhaps the most fundamental and immediately obvious of these is the incorrect lead.

Outward signs of tractability and insufficient tractability, from Knopfhart's Dressage A Guidebook for the Road to Success.

Wrong Lead

There is a very strong consensus among the Masters that wrong lead in young or partly schooled horses is not an overt disobedience and does not deserve punishment. Alois Podhajsky emphasises the different response to wrong lead from a young horse, as compared to that of a highly trained horse.

If the horse strikes off on the wrong leg…the rider should allow him to continue for a few strides before bringing him back to a trot and trying another strike-off. On no account must he bring the horse to an immediate halt, which would result in confusion and fear. This is one of the many differences between training the young horse and the school horse. The latter, as a punishment for a wrong strike-off, should be stopped immediately and made to strike off again.

    Alois Podhajsky *The Complete Training of Horse and Rider*

It may be noteworthy that the punishment here is simply a correction. Podhajsky also emphasises that difficulties with a certain lead will not be resolved by the rider taking the easy option:

The necessity of cantering equally on both leads must be underlined, as some riders are inclined to work more on the lead on which the horse finds the canter easier. The development of one side more than the other would create difficulties in the course of training.

    Alois Podhajsky *The Complete Training of Horse and Rider*

Underlying physical difficulties – which will not be resolved by force – are cited as the likely cause of problems:

Horses that frequently strike out on the wrong lead should also not be forced in any way since this phenomenon is usually based on natural crookedness which cannot be overcome so quickly in this phase of the horse's training. Only cross-cantering [cantering disunited] must not be permitted.

    Gustav Steinbrecht *Gymnasium of the Horse*

Reiner Klimke makes the point that the rider's aiding can either diminish the underlying difficulty, or add to it:

We must not be surprised if the young horse strikes off on the wrong leg sometimes. Most horses have a weaker and a stronger side. As a rule the young horse finds it easier to canter on the left leg, as its natural crookedness means that the left hind leg can support weight more easily than the right. We therefore first use the diagonal aids to straighten the horse on its difficult side before asking for canter. We also check whether we ourselves have given the correct aids or perhaps collapsed the hip.

Reiner Klimke *Basic Training of the Young Horse*

Far from reacting in a negative way to a wrong lead, Erik Herbermann suggests that it can be turned to advantage:

Should the horse strike-off on the wrong lead...we mustn't get rough with it, snatching it back sharply to the trot or walk. Instead, we can use this mistake to our advantage...We can ride the counter-canter for a few moments *deliberately;* it will help to supple the horse. Then patiently bring it through the downward transition, and after a few moments of better preparation try the correct lead again. Only adequate preparation (suppling, balancing) will produce the correct lead consistently.

He adds, in a footnote:

This presupposes, of course, that the rider's seat and aids are correct. Most canter errors can be directly traced to false seat influences. Erik Herbermann *Dressage Formula*

The rider's role in establishing the desired lead is explored with wry humour by Henry Wynmalen:

We, in studying these starts at the canter, are no doubt attempting to polish the use of our aids, to make them finer and lighter; we may be concerned also with straightening them. It follows that occasions must arise when our aids, or what we intended to be our aids, are misunderstood by the horse, causing him to strike off on what we will consider the wrong leg. Such misunderstandings are neither ill-will nor disobedience on the part of the horse; it is even conceivable that we ourselves have not been very clear in expressing our wishes! Obviously, then, any form of punishment, roughness or even impatience are out of the question.

Henry Wynmalen *Dressage A Study of the Finer Points of Riding*

It may be appropriate to follow these words of Wynmalen's with an observation by Major-General Geoffrey Brooke. As mentioned earlier, Brooke was one Weedon officer who did not subscribe to the exterior lateral aids which Wynmalen so detested. Whilst Brooke did not consider himself to be an authority on high school dressage, he was a highly perceptive and practical all-round horseman, who had to make the best of the horses at his disposal.

Possibly from being badly schooled in the first place a horse will strongly resent cantering with a particular leg leading. Let us assume that he refuses to lead with the off-fore. Trot him along the side of an incline, with the slope upward on your right. Apply the diagonal aid for leading with the off-fore and he will lead with this leg in preference to the other leg on the downhill side. Geoffrey Brooke *Horsemanship Dressage & Show-Jumping*

In making such use of natural terrain, Brooke is following a legacy of many great Masters, for whom 'schooling' was never an occupation necessarily confined to the school. In fact, the value of using sloping natural terrain to improve what would generally be considered 'dressage' (i.e. school) movements is described by a number of the greatest authorities on equitation.

Disunited

The disunited canter, and the reasons for it, are explained by Alois Podhajsky...

A common fault with weak horses is the disunited canter, in which the horse canters with the left leg leading in front and the right leg leading behind, or vice versa. The rider will be able to recognise the fault by an uncomfortable feeling through the horse's back.

Alois Podhajsky *The Complete Training of Horse and Rider*

...and Erik Herbermann:

Disunited or cross-canter occurs when the horse switches its lead behind (or in front) only...This usually happens because the rider's seat is tense or unquiet, or the outside leg is not held clearly back (supporting the quarters), or because of imbalance or tensions in the horse. Erik Herbermann *Dressage Formula*

Although these two writers emphasise different reasons for disunited canter, these reasons are not mutually exclusive, and a common factor is that none is the horse's *fault:*

It is most important that the horse should never be made to feel that a change of lead or going disunited are 'punishable faults'…as it would then be very difficult later on to obtain changes of lead and to eradicate from the horse's memory the punishment which he would expect to receive.

General Decarpentry *Academic Equitation*

Crookedness

A contributory factor in some cases of wrong lead, crookedness is probably the most prevalent fault in canter. In fact, it can properly be described as an inherent fault, which only correct training can eradicate:

In this gait, the horse is not naturally straight, and his obliqueness in relation to the direction of his progress is seldom the same on both leads….

Absolute straightness in the whole length of the body is never natural to the horse at any pace because of congenital asymmetry, but it is at the canter that the bend is most pronounced, and the task of straightening him at this gait is especially difficult…

Usually, the horse which is naturally inflexed to the left…canters in a relatively straight position on the right lead. The legs of his right diagonal will both be placed more or less on the line of the course. Those of the other diagonal will be placed on either side of this line, but with the hind leg further away from it than the foreleg. In this case, the natural bend of the horse counteracts the crookedness peculiar to the canter on the right lead, and therefore produces relative straightness.

On the contrary, on the left lead, the two deviations add up, and the horse is seen to go markedly crooked as well as bent.

General Decarpentry *Academic Equitation*

A horse with a natural bend to the left, cantering on the right lead.

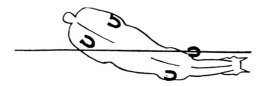

A horse with a natural bend to the left, cantering on the left lead.

Illustrations of crookedness from Decarpentry's Academic Equitation.

John Winnett analyses the effects of natural crookedness in very similar terms:

Of the three gaits, the canter is the most difficult for the horse to find his balance under the rider, the fundamental problems being the horse's rectitude and the stiffness in his hind legs. Let us examine the problems of a horse who is...convex on his right lateral, and concave on his left lateral. When, during the first phase of training we ask this horse to canter on his left lead, we will observe that the horse's concavity places his haunches to the left (inside) and, because of stiffness in his strong right hind, he transfers his croup even farther to the inside. We are therefore confronted with two problems; one of inflexion from a problem of rectitude and one of deviation from a strong, stiff right hind. Cantering on the right lead, however, will not pose such a problem because the horse's right lateral is convex, and thrusts from his left hind are weaker. Therefore, we will not observe as much inflexion and deviation to the right (inside).

John Winnett *Dressage as Art in Competition*

Even if the problem of crookedness is generally less evident in right canter, it was still observed by de la Guérinière, who promptly prescribed his newly devised exercise of shoulder-in as the remedy:

The horse should gallop in the posture of the shoulder-in, not only to render it more supple and obedient, but also to prevent the bad habit, shown by nearly all horses, of galloping with the inside hind leg outside the line of the inside foreleg. This fault is not inconsiderable, for it gives the rider an uneasy seat, as can easily be seen in the case of most gallops, e.g. on the right leg, which is the way hunting and work horses gallop. You will notice that they nearly always have the left shoulder drawn back, and they incline somewhat to the left. The reason is not far to seek: the horse, while galloping with the right leg swinging away from the left, jostles the rider towards the outside. For this reason the horse must gallop shoulder-in, to teach it to keep the hind legs close to one another and to lower the hindquarters. When the animal has been suppled and broken of this false posture, it can easily gallop with united hindquarters, which is the proper form of the gallop.

* Nowadays, when cantering in the open, while we may give thought to occasionally varying the leading leg, we do not think of one or other lead as being 'correct' or 'incorrect'. However, de la Guérinière's comment here, and the following extract from the same work, suggests that this was not always so:

Gallop to the left

False gallop to the left

Gallop to the left, disunited in the forehand

Gallop to the left, disunited behind

(And opposite) Various forms of canter, from de la Guérinière's School of Horsemanship.

It should be remarked that for horses destined for the hunt and the cavalry, the term leading on the proper leg means – particularly in France – leading on the right leg. Nonetheless,

Gallop to the right   False gallop to the right

Gallop to the left   False gallop to the left

there are horsemen who cause their horses to change hand, in order to ease the left leg, which bears the greatest stress because it carries all the weight, whereas the right leg begins the gait, enjoys greater freedom from burden and hence does not so quickly become fatigued.

François Robichon de la Guérinière *School of Horsemanship*

Furthermore, the idea of there being a 'correct' leading leg is not so archaic as might be supposed. Here is an extract from *Breaking and Riding*, first published in 1902:

We ought always to begin the canter with the off fore leading [footnote: The rule for riding is to begin all movements to the right. On a straight line in the open we generally canter with the off fore leading, which is the style adopted by ladies [side-saddle]...ladies do not like to canter to the left because it displaces their seat too much.]

James Fillis *Breaking and Riding*

Breaking and Riding contains an interesting observation on the stresses placed upon the limbs in canter. Whereas de la Guérinière comments on the relative roles of the forelimbs, Fillis has this to say about the hind limbs:

Fig. 43.—First time of the canter ; near hind in support.

Fig. 44.—Second time of the canter ; left diagonal in support.

Fig. 45. — Third time of the canter ; off fore in support.

The three times of canter, from Fillis's Breaking and Riding

It might appear...that the near hind is the leg which becomes most fatigued at a canter to the right. In fact, this is the usual opinion of many...who have written on the subject. Nothing could be more erroneous; because the off hock, being under the body and having to raise all the weight, does the most work during each stride, which is a fact beyond dispute. I am aware that the near hock, being placed at the end of the arm of the lever, is under a much less favourable condition for action. But precisely because the position which the off hock occupies under the body, is more favourable to the complete utilisation of its force, it makes a greater effort than the near hock, and consequently it becomes more fatigued. If we attentively watch a horse which is cantering with his off fore leading, we will quickly see that the off hock and fetlock become much more bent than the near ones, and consequently their upward action is better marked and their spring more energetic.

If we canter to the right a horse which has an unsound off hock, caused, for instance, by a spavin or a curb, he will immediately become disunited, on account of the movement causing him pain. But if we make him canter with the near fore leading, he will not change his hind legs.

The off hock therefore exerts more force in the canter to the right, and the near hock in the canter to the left. On this account, the rider ought to keep his legs firmly closed, especially during the second period [diagonal support] of the canter. By doing this, the hock, which is under the body, is quickened in its action, the horse is pressed forward...if we do not act thus, the second period will be slower and heavier than the other two.

James Fillis *Breaking and Riding*

Ulrik Schramm, whose writing concentrates upon resolving schooling problems, points out the role of the inside hind in maximising or minimising crookedness in canter. His remedy combines use of shoulder-fore with the astute application of the aids: he presumably emphasises the rider's inside leg aid for the same reason as Decarpentry – because significant pressure from the outside leg might cause the hindquarters to deviate to the inside even more:

A horse will always strike off to canter with its hindquarters turned in if the rider cannot make it engage its inside hind to get it to balance and propel the mass efficiently. After a crooked strike off, the subsequent strides of the canter will always lack expressive quality and collection will be impossible to achieve.

The irregularity would not become established if we always ensured a straight strike-off to canter either from the trot or from the walk. To start with, we must ride on a circle and enlarge it over one or two strides, thus putting the horse in a very modest degree of shoulder-in (shoulder-fore) position; this will constrain the horse to support our weight properly with its inside hind; we can then give the indication to canter with our inside leg. If we have already acquired a well-balanced and feeling seat, we will be able to ensure the precise moment at which our horse can respond to the cantering aid of our inside leg; if we still lack the ability to feel the right moment, we must at least know that the inside leg must act at the moment when the outside hind comes into support, giving the inside hind freedom to swing forward powerfully; we can then be guided by observation of the horse's shoulders.   Ulrik Schramm *The Undisciplined Horse*

The issue of crookedness and the basic remedy are summarised in succinct fashion by Erik Herbermann:

During any canter work we must keep the horse truly straight. Most horses tend to evade the honest loading of the inside hind leg by bringing the quarters toward the inside; it is a very common occurrence. For sufficiently advanced riders, it is helpful to ride the horse in a *slight* shoulder-fore position as a correction for the 'croup-in syndrome'.

Erik Herbermann Dressage Formula

While Üdo Burger provides a timely reminder that...

...it is only if there is enough impulsion that the horse is perfectly straight in the canter. It is quite impossible to have a horse straight at a lolloping sort of canter.

Üdo Burger The Way to Perfect Horsemanship

Other Faults

In his book, *Dressage as Art in Competition,* John Winnett describes various faults in the canter. While some of his text relates primarily to the gait variants and/or the specific demands of test movements, he also deals with more general issues, including the following:

Four-beat rhythm. This fault can originate from poor rectitude, stiffness, and lack of strength in the hindquarters and back...only further gymnastic work in the trot can improve the situation. Horses that persist in cantering in four beats, after extensive gymnastic training in the trot, will never overcome this fault altogether...

Horses who show a faster tempo on one lead than the other. This...is always a fault of rectitude and can best be corrected on circles. Let us assume that we are dealing with a horse who is dominant right and the rhythm of his canter is faster on the left lead. To correct this problem I place the horse on a large circle to the right and ride a lively working canter on the right lead, after which I counter-canter this circle on the left lead to develop maximum thrust from the right hind leg.

Horses who canter wide behind. This problem is often observed in stallions, or in horses who are built wide behind, or are outright bow-legged. These horses disengage their hind legs, raise their croups, transfer weight to their forehand, fall out of balance, and in extreme cases use the rider's hand as a 'fifth leg'. Such horses have to be ridden on 8 metre circles and voltes…They must not be allowed to lose rhythm or impulsion on the circles. When cantering on straight lines, they must be kept constantly in shoulder-in. I have used renvers and travers canter from time to time with such horses, but I have always found that shoulder-in is best, for it allows complete control over the inside hind leg, and helps in regaining engagement, balance and straightness.

John Winnett *Dressage as Art in Competition*

Rider Errors

As with all aspects of equitation there are, of course, many overt errors of rider posture and aid application that will compromise the quality of the canter. Here, Henry Wynmalen concentrates on the relative roles of the outside and inside leg:

…there is nothing more unsightly than a horse which swings his quarters sideways each time he is given the office to canter. He will only acquire a tendency to do so if the rider applies his outside leg too far back or pushes it, as for a side-step. It is wrong to do that, because the aid for the canter is 'closing' the leg and not pushing with it! And, of course, the rider's inside leg must also see to it that the animal be always maintained in a straight position.   Henry Wynmalen *Equitation*

While the faults noted by John Winnett...

The main rider errors in the canter are failure to obtain response to the inside leg, and not giving with the fingers on the reins at the end of the third beat before the time of suspension. The horse must not be restrained at this moment; he must be free to jump forward.   John Winnett *Dressage as Art in Competition*

...go right to the heart of Steinbrecht's maxim: 'Ride the horse forward and set it straight'.

Conclusion

Further work at canter will entail development of the gait variants and counter-canter, flying changes and lateral movements – subject matter for other titles in this series. Canter is, of course, also the gait upon which most forms of jumping are based.

If the trot is universally acknowledged as the primary utilitarian gait, then the complex, demanding and potentially beautiful canter might be described at the primary aesthetic gait. Certainly, it is the gait in which the horse can appear balletic – pirouetting, dancing in zigzags and tempi changes and flying over huge obstacles. However, such things will be possible only if great attention is given to correct basic training. As Wynmalen says:

Complete calm and peacefulness are important in all stages of training the horse, but never more so than in this work at canter. There is no other work which can upset and spoil a horse more thoroughly and more quickly than an injudicious approach to the inherent difficulties of this gait.

It is essential to seek response to discreet and careful aids and it is essential in particular to find that response without the use of any force, ever. The better, the more generous and the more high-couraged one's horse, the more carefully one has to proceed.

Henry Wynmalen *Dressage A Study of the Finer Points of Riding*

Bibliography

Many of the books cited in this work have been produced in numerous editions, sometimes by more than one publisher. Some, indeed, have been subject to various translations into different languages. Listed below are the editions which have been referred to during the compilation of this book. Where appropriate, information on first publication has been added, to help place the works in historical context.

Albrecht, Kurt, *A Dressage Judge's Handbook*, J.A. Allen (London) 1988
  Principles of Dressage, J.A. Allen (London) 1993. (1st edn. Verlag ORAC, Vienna 1981).
Baucher, François, *New Method of Horsemanship*, in *François Baucher the Man and his Method*, Hilda Nelson, J.A. Allen (London) 1992. (First published as *Méthode d'Equitation basée sur de nouveaux principes*, France 1842.)
Belasik, Paul, *Riding Towards the Light*, J.A. Allen (London) 1990.
Burger, Üdo, *The Way to Perfect Horsemanship* (tr. Nicole Bartle), J.A. Allen (London) 1998. (First published as *Vollendete Reitkunst*, Paul Parey, Berlin and Hamburg 1959.)
Brooke, Maj.-Gen. Geoffrey, *Horsemanship Dressage & Show-Jumping*, Seeley, Service & Co. Ltd. (London) 1968 (1st edn. 1929).

Decarpentry, Gen., *Academic Equitation* (tr. Nicole Bartle), J.A. Allen (London) 1987. (First published in France 1949).

De la Guérinière, François Robichon, *School of Horsemanship* (tr. Tracy Boucher), J.A. Allen (London) 1994. (First published in a single volume as *Ecole de Cavalerie,* Paris 1733.)

d'Endrödy, Lt. Col. A.L., *Give Your Horse a Chance,* J.A. Allen (London) 1989 (First edn. 1959).

Felton, W. Sidney, *Masters of Equitation,* J.A. Allen (London) 1962.

Fillis, James, *Breaking and Riding,* J.A. Allen (London) 1986. (First English edn. 1902.)

Harris, Charles, *Fundamentals of Riding,* J.A. Allen (London) 1985.

Herbermann, Erik, *Dressage Formula* (3rd edn.), J.A.Allen (London) 1999.

Klimke, Reiner, *Basic Training of the Young Horse* (tr. Sigrid Young), J.A. Allen (London) 1994. (First published as *Grundausbildung des jungen Reitpferdes,* Franckh'sche Verlagshandlung, Stuttgart 1984.)

L'Hotte, Gen. Alexis-François, *Questions Équestres* (tr. Hilda Nelson in *Alexis-François L'Hotte The Quest For Lightness In Equitation),* J.A. Allen (London) 1997. (*Questions Équestres* first published in France, 1906.)

Jousseaume, André, *Progressive Dressage* (tr. Jeanette Vigneron), J.A. Allen (London) 1978. (First published in France by Émile Hazan.)

Müseler, Wilhelm, *Riding Logic* (tr. F.W. Schiller), Eyre Methuen Ltd. (London) 1975. (First published as *Müseler: RERT'LEHRE,* Paul Parey Verlag, Berlin and Hamburg pre. 1937.)

Oliveira, Nuno, *Reflections on Equestrian Art* (tr. Phyllis Field), J.A. Allen (London) 1988. (First published as *Reflexions sur l'Art Equestre,* Crépin Leblond, France 1964.)

Notes and Reminiscences of a Portuguese Rider, special publication 1982.

Podhajsky, Alois, *The Complete Training of Horse and Rider* (tr. Eva Podhajsky), The Sportsman's Press (London) 1997. (First published as *Die Klassiche Reitkunst,* Nymphenburger Verlagshand-lung GmbH., Munich 1965.)

Schramm, Ulrik, *The Undisciplined Horse* (tr. Nicole Bartle), J.A. Allen (London) 1986. (First published as *Das verrittene Pferd – Ursachen und Weg der Korrektur,* BLV Verlagsgesellschaft, Munich 1983.)

Seunig, Waldemar, *Horsemanship* (tr. Leonard Mins), Robert Hale (London) 1958. (First published in Germany 1941.)

  The Essence of Horsemanship (tr. Jacqueline Stirlin Harris), J.A. Allen (London) 1986. (First published in Germany by Erich Hoffmann Verlag 1961.)

Steinbrecht, Gustav, *The Gymnasium of the Horse* (tr. from German 10th edn. Helen K. Buckle), Xenophon Press (Ohio) 1995. (First published in Germany 1885.)

Wätjen, Richard L., *Dressage Riding* (tr. Dr V. Saloschin), J.A. Allen (London) 1973. (First published in Germany 1958.)

Winnett, John, *Dressage as Art in Competition,* J.A. Allen (London) 1993.

Wynmalen, Henry, *Dressage A Study of the Finer Points of Riding,* Wilshire Book Company (California) (First published in 1952.)

  Equitation, J.A. Allen (London) 1971. (First edn. 1938.)

Biographies of Quoted Masters

The following are brief biographies of those whose works are cited in this book. They are given both for reasons of general interest and to assist the reader in placing each author in historical and cultural context.

Albrecht, Kurt Born in Austria in 1920, Albrecht chose a military career and saw active service as an Artillery Commander in the Second World War, before becoming a prisoner of war in Russia. After the war, he joined the Austrian Constabulary and taught equitation at the Constabulary Central School.

Albrecht was a great friend of Hans Handler and, when Handler succeeded Alois Podhajsky as Director of the Spanish Riding School, Albrecht joined the School to assist with administration, being appointed Substitute Director in 1965. In 1974 he succeeded Handler as Director, a post he held until 1985.

From 1973 until 1987 Albrecht was in charge of judges' affairs for the Austrian Equestrian Federation, subsequently playing a leading role in equestrian educational advancement.

Baucher, François (1796–1873) A highly controversial figure, who rode entirely in the school, Baucher began his career under the tutelage of his uncle, director of stables to the

Governor of Milan. Whilst in Italy, he would have witnessed the practices of the old Neapolitan school, which were still dominant in that country.

In 1816, political upheaval saw Baucher's return to France, where he managed and taught in several private manèges. In 1834, he moved to Paris and established a relationship with the fashionable Franconi circus. Riding haute école in the circus gave Baucher the prestige he yearned, and in 1842 he published his 'new method' *(Méthode d'Equitation basée sur de nouveaux principes).*

In 1855, Baucher was badly injured when the chandelier of an indoor school fell on him. Thereafter, he never performed in public again, although he remained able to do some riding and teaching. In later life, he became very reflective and appears to have modified some of his earlier ideas.

The controversy that surrounded Baucher's writing and teaching is well documented in Hilda Nelson's *François Baucher the Man and his Method,* in which the author writes: 'The goal of Baucher's method is the total disposition of the horse's strength and the total submission of the horse to the will of the horseman.' What is beyond question is that Baucher trained a number of dangerous horses to perform advanced movements in a remarkably short time, and Fillis said of him: 'He had the great merit of not describing anything which he could not do.'

Baucher remains respected by many eminent authorities and his reputation is believed by some to have been compromised by equestrian politics, the limitations of his own powers of expression, and the insensitivity of his translators.

Belasik, Paul Born in Buffalo, New York in 1950, Belasik showed a strong affinity with animals from childhood. Early interests included monkey breeding and falconry, as well as horses. This diversity of interest extended beyond the animal kingdom – entering Cornell University as part of the pre-veterinary programme, he graduated with a science degree and had, in the meantime, won prizes for his painting and become a published poet.

By the time of his graduation in 1971, Belasik's career as a horseman had already begun; he taught college courses, evented and competed in dressage at all levels. However, never really excited by competition, he began to focus more on an in-depth study of equitation for its own sake. Initially involved in breeding and training German horses, he focused first upon the German system, broadening and deepening his studies to encompass the different schools of riding. He cites as major influences H.L.M. van Schaik, who instilled in him a love of the classicists and Nuno Oliveira, with whom he spent some time in Portugal. His interest in the philosophical aspects of equitation has been augmented by studies of Zen Buddhism and the martial arts.

Belasik owns and operates a training stable in Pennsylvania, where he works with a broad-based clientele including international competitors, and riders of all levels who have no interest in competition. He also holds clinics and lectures on a national and international basis.

Burger, Üdo (1914–1980) One of Germany's most respected veterinary surgeons and animal psychologists, Burger was an accomplished horseman and a highly respected judge. Involved with horses from an early age, he was reputed to become fretful if unable to spend some time each day in their company. Very obviously a horse lover, he wrote (without giving specific detail) that a horse had actually saved his life in wartime. His professional skills gave him a profound understanding of both the horse's movement and motivation, and he could be blunt in his criticism of rough riding, and of those who made insufficient effort to understand the horse's nature.

Brooke, Maj.-Gen. Geoffrey (1884–1966) Brooke was a genuine all-round horseman. His book *Horsemanship Dressage & Show-Jumping* includes chapters on racing over fences and polo. As a Lt. Colonel he was, in the 1920s, Chief Instructor to the British Cavalry School at Weedon, at a time when British equitation was undergoing a modernising transformation under European influences. A keen student of equitation, he might fairly be described as one of the figures who helped to move British equitation forward.

Decarpentry, General (1878–1956) Born at Lambres, the son and grandson of enthusiastic pupils of François Baucher, Decarpentry soon decided upon a career in the cavalry. Wounded in action at Verdun, he dismissed the permanent damage to his left elbow, saying that it kept his arm bent in the correct position for riding. The injury had no adverse affect on his career, since he was to become commander of cavalry at Saint-Cyr and second in command of the Cadré Noir (1925–31).

From 1939 onward, Decarpentry acted as judge at many international dressage competitions. He also presided over the FEI jury and became President of the FEI Dressage Committee, in which role he was highly influential in developing an international consensus on the aims and judging of competition dressage.

As a rider and equestrian thinker, Decarpentry was by no means confined by the Baucheriste influences of his childhood, as both the references cited in Academic Equitation, and his own text shows. It is also evident that he took innovative advantage of the then-young techniques of cinematography to help analyse equine movement.

Decarpentry was a modest man and, although held in great esteem as a rider, he had no desire to participate in competition, his legacy being the skill of his instruction, his work in developing the FEI and the integrity and scholarship which he applied to his equestrian writing.

De la Guérinière, François Robichon (c.1688–1751) Widely regarded as the most influential figure in equestrian history, de la Guérinière was born in Essay, the son of a lawyer. A pupil of Antoine de Vendeuil, he also had a brother who ran a riding academy in Caen. In 1715, de la Guérinière was granted the title of *écuyer de roi,* and opened a riding academy in Paris, apparently under licence from the Duc d'Anjou.

At his Parisian academy, de la Guérinière taught not only riding, but what was described as 'the complete science of the horse'. By 1730 his reputation was such that he was given the Directorship of the Académie des Tuileries. Despite phenomenal success as a teacher, de la Guérinière was unable to run the academy profitably, and struggled constantly with money – a fact which might endear him to modern-day equestrians.

De la Guérinière's legacy was to develop, from the older style of classical riding, a freedom of movement which characterises modern classical equitation – an achievement which has led him to be described as the 'first of the modern classical riders' (W.S. Felton) and 'undoubtedly the father of modern equitation' (Wynmalen). His lucid work *Ecole de Cavalerie* is quite remarkable for its timeless relevance and wisdom, and continues to be a source of reference for many present-day authorities.

d'Endrödy, Lt. Col. A.L. (1902–1988) A native of Hungary, a country with a great equestrian heritage, d'Endrödy was a member of the Royal Hungarian Olympic three-day event team in 1936, a member of the Hungarian international showjumping team and a champion amateur race rider. The basic idea for *Give Your Horse a Chance* was formulated during the fourteen years which d'Enrödy spent at Orkenytabor, the Hungarian Academy for riding instructors and the training ground for their Olympic team. The book itself was drafted during the three and a half ('sad, lonely') years in which he was a prisoner of war in Russian hands, and it may be that the depth of detail in the book is partially attributable to this period of incarceration.

One of d'Endrödy's major influences was as the trainer of Bertalan de Nemethy, coach to the USA Olympic equestrian team in a golden era that produced riders such as William Steinkraus – a great equestrian scholar, who helped refine the translation of *Give Your Horse a Chance* and provided the preface. Largely through his meeting with Col. Frank Weldon at the Stockholm Olympics (where Weldon captained the victorious British Team), d'Endrödy also had a considerable impact on equitation in Britain and spent some time at Badminton, as a guest of the Duke of Beaufort.

Felton, W. Sidney The author of the informative work quoted in the preliminary pages of this book, Felton was born in Massachusetts in 1895. A graduate of Harvard Law School, he served as a US Aviation Officer in the First World War, and subsequently practised law in Boston. A lifelong rider and highly analytical equestrian scholar, he was a keen follower of hounds, an amateur instructor and judge and a leading figure in the organisation of the US Pony Club. Felton was well respected by many leading riders of his era, and the foreword for his *Masters of Equitation* was provided by Henry Wynmalen.

Fillis, James (1834–1913) Born in London, Fillis went to France at an early age. There he met François Baucher and, greatly impressed by his methods, studied them under Baucher's pupil, François Caron. (Later in life, Fillis found himself at odds with some of Baucher's ideas – as his Commentaries on Baucher in Breaking and Riding show – but he always retained an overall admiration for him.)

After running his own school in Le Havre, Fillis moved to Paris, where he supervised the stables of various members of the nobility. Then, wishing to promote his method more widely, he followed the same course as Baucher, and began to perform in the circus, to great acclaim. Pressed to produce a book, Fillis was offered editorial assistance by a long-time pupil, the French politician, Clemenceau. Published in 1890, the book was subsequently translated into English by the eminent veterinary author, Horace Hayes.

From 1891–7, Fillis was based in Germany. He then went to Russia with Circus Ciniselli and created such an impression that he was offered, and accepted, the post of Colonel and *Ecuyer-en-chef* of the Russian Cavalry School – a position he held until retiring in 1910. During his period of office, a visiting American Army Commission decided to adopt his method, and *Breaking and Riding* became the official textbook of the US Cavalry School.

Interestingly, given that he was active only a century ago, Fillis totally disapproved of women riding astride!

Harris, Charles (b. 1915) An engineer by profession, Charles Harris qualified as a riding instructor in 1932 and went on to become a Fellow of the Institute of the Horse, a Fellow of the British Horse Society and a Fellow of the Association of British Riding Schools.

From 1948–51, through the support of Col. V.D.S. Williams, he became the first and only English rider to complete the full three-year course at the Spanish Riding School. Here, he trained under Commandants Alois Podhajsky and Hans Handler, and with such luminaries as Rochowansky, Lindenbauer and Wahl.

A fervent devotee of classical principles, Charles Harris is an advocate of using correct equestrian terminology to ensure that these principles are conveyed precisely and concisely to pupils and students of equitation, and his many writings reflect this fact.

Herbermann, Erik Born in Amsterdam in 1945, Herbermann moved at an early age with his family to Johannesburg and ten years later, moved to Canada. His initial equestrian training was with Patricia Salt FBHS, herself a pupil of Richard Wätjen and Oberbereiter Lindenbauer at the Spanish Riding School. Herbermann subsequently studied under the celebrated classical riding teacher, Egon von Neindorff.

Now residing in the USA, Herbermann devotes much of his time to lecturing, teaching and conducting clinics internationally. As well as producing three editions of *Dressage Formula,* he has also written numerous articles for equestrian publications.

Herbermann is a staunch advocate of classical ideals, and his ideology is based on an objective study of the horse's nature, which seeks the depth of understanding and quality of work perceived in the greatest of Renaissance Masters. In common with these luminaries, he views equitation as a self-improving art, rooted in the utmost affection and respect for the horse.

Jousseaume, André (d. 1960) A graduate of Saumur and a cavalry officer for most of his lifetime, Jousseaume won the individual silver medal for dressage at the 1932 Olympics when a member of the French gold medal winning team, and repeated this feat in both respects in 1948. He also took the bronze medal in 1952. He retired from the French army with the rank of Colonel and taught at the *Cercle Hippique* until his death.

Klimke, Reiner (1936–1999) Born in Munster, Germany, Klimke began his association with horses when, evacuated to a farm during the war years, he journeyed to school by horse and cart. After the war, he took lessons at Herr Stecken's Westphalian Riding School and, in 1953, he came to the notice of Gustav Rau, who did much to revive Germany's equestrian fortunes in the post-war era. Rau invited Klimke to train at Warendorf, where for three years his roommate was the great showjumper, Alwin Schockemöhle. At that time Schockemöhle was concentrating on eventing but, in 1956, he decided that his future lay in showjumping, and passed the ride on his horse, Lausbub, to Klimke – who promptly won team silver at the 1957 European Three Day Event Championships. Two years later, Klimke won team gold at these championships on Fortunat.

By this time, Klimke was also achieving considerable success in dressage, and his career was under way. Having studied law from 1955, he became a fully qualified lawyer in 1964. With the demands of his profession to consider, he decided that he could more readily combine this with his equestrian activities if he concentrated upon dressage rather than eventing. This decision saw the start of a long and immensely successful period of international competition revolving mainly, but not exclusively, around the great horses Dux, Mehmed and Ahlerich. During a period spanning three decades Klimke, as an individual, won an Olympic gold medal, two World Championships and four European Championships, and was a member of teams that won Germany gold medals at six Olympics, six World Championships and thirteen European Championships.

L'Hotte, Gen. Alexis-François (1825–1904) A son and grandson of French cavalrymen, L'Hotte was, from an early age, a keen student of the equestrian writings of the old French Masters – much to the detriment of his academic education. He initially attended the military academy of Saint-Cyr as a young cadet, being sent on to pursue his equestrian interests at Saumur, since the cavalry section at Saint-Cyr had been closed. Despite some youthful indiscipline, he eventually attained the rank of General, and became Commandant of the re-opened cavalry section at Saint-Cyr, and subsequently of Saumur.

It is of great interest to students of equestrian history that L'Hotte was a pupil of both François Baucher and Comte D'Aure, two highly influential figures who not only practised different styles of equitation, but were considered rivals and had their own factions of supporters. L'Hotte was a great note-taker, and his anecdotes about and comparisons of these two figures make fascinating reading.

L'Hotte himself was considered to be one of the most outstanding *écuyers* of a golden age: he originated the phrase 'equestrian tact' and the famous maxim 'calm, forward and straight'.

Müseler, Wilhelm (1887–1952) Born in Berlin, Müseler was, in his youth, a fine athlete – he held the German record for the

100m sprint. Following a grammar school education, he embarked upon a career as a cavalry officer. During the years preceding the First World War, he competed with great success at dressage and showjumping, and was a member of the German Olympic equestrian team. However, upon being told by his commanding officer that he should make his career 'with his intellect rather than his backside', he intensified his commitment to his primary role as an officer. His military abilities are evidenced by the fact that, by 1918, he had become the youngest Major on the General Staff. Later in life, when recalled to the General Staff at the onset of World War II, he was to attain the rank of General.

Leaving the army after the end of the First World War, Müseler again committed himself to equitation, becoming Director of Tattersall Beermann, then the largest equestrian centre in Berlin. In this role, his emphasis shifted away from active competition and towards training horses and riders and organising equestrian events. He also became Master of the Berlin Hunting Society and President of the German Association of Hunting Clubs.

In 1931, health problems compelled him to cease his riding activities. *Riding Logic*, written by way of a conclusion, was originally intended for the academic equestrian societies he had founded. Once published, however, the book became a bestseller, appearing in many editions and many languages. From 1932 onward, Müseler also wrote books on the history of art, one of which sold over a million copies – he considered these books the most important work of his life.

Oliveira, Nuno (d.1989) This great Portuguese Master began his career as a pupil of Joaquin Gonzales de Miranda, former Master of the Horse to the Portuguese Royal Family. After

Miranda's death, Oliveira trained horses first for cavalry officers and a dealer, then for one of Miranda's pupils, Senõr Chefalenez. Subsequently, a friend and student, Manuel de Barros asked him to train at his brother-in-law's stud where, in addition to having many good horses to ride, he also had at his disposal a large equestrian library. During this period, he met Alois Podhajsky when they both rode at an exhibition in the Campo Grande and the pair became firm friends.

During the 1950s, Oliveira attracted a number of highly talented pupils, and opened his riding school at Quinta do Chafaris. He also began to write articles (and subsequently, books) on equitation, while a pupil organised a weekly TV programme showing his lessons.

In 1961 he gave his first exhibition abroad, in Switzerland, and the following year he rode in the Winter Circus in Paris, where he met and established a lasting relationship with Capt. Durand, later to be Commander of the Cadre Noir.

Subsequent years saw a further influx of pupils, many from abroad, and numerous clinics and exhibitions throughout Europe, North and South America and Australia, which continued up to the time of his death.

Podhajsky, Alois (1899–1973) The son of an Austro-Hungarian cavalry officer, Podhajsky joined a dragoon regiment aged seventeen and received regular lessons from Capt. Count Telekei, whom he described as an excellent instructor.

Although in a cavalry regiment, Podhajsky spent much of the First World War on foot. After the war, following the demise of the Austro-Hungarian Empire, he was admitted to the new Federal Army, and riding once again became part of his career. Having achieved considerable success in showjumping, he was encouraged by his colonel to study dressage, which he found further improved his horse's jumping. Transferred to advanced training at the cavalry school at Schlosshof, he began to achieve international success in dressage, showjumping and three-day events.

In 1933, he was sent to the Spanish Riding School, where he studied under luminaries such as Polak, Zrust and Lindenbauer. Their influence helped him to train his own horses to Grand Prix level and to win a bronze medal for dressage at the 1936 Olympics.

From 1934–8 he worked as a cavalry instructor, first in Austria and then in Germany. In 1938 Austria was annexed by Germany, and the Spanish Riding School was placed under the command of the German Army. When, in 1939, Podhajsky became Director of the Spanish Riding School, he managed to convince senior German officers, who were experienced horsemen, of the value of the School. By this, and other actions in that period, Podhajsky was instrumental in protecting the School for posterity.

In the post-war years, Podhajsky competed abroad both with his own horses and the School's Lipizzaners. He also took the Spanish Riding School on a number of foreign tours, including a major tour of the USA shortly before his retirement in 1964.

Schramm, Ulrik (1912–1995) A vastly experienced German horseman and equestrian author, who was dedicated to the proper education of horses for all disciplines. His philosophy is expounded in his own words: 'Seat is obviously an essential element in mastery of the horse, but the rider's head is surely as important as his seat'; 'Riding is not truly a sport if unity of mind does not exist between rider and horse.' A talented artist, Schramm used his own mild caricatures of horses and riders to emphasise the points made in his writing.

Seunig, Waldemar (1887–1976) Born in the then Duchy of Krain, Seunig was educated at a military academy in Austria and entered the cavalry. He subsequently attended the Riding Instructors' Institute in Vienna, where he became a pupil of the famous Josipovich. Then, in the political upheaval of the times, he was more or less repatriated (to what was by that time Slovenia, in Yugoslavia).

Since, by then, he had established a considerable reputation, he was offered the post of Master of the Horse at the Yugoslavian Royal Court. This he accepted, on condition that he first spent a year at the French Cavalry School at Saumur, and six months at the Royal Mews in London (to learn protocol). Subsequently, he was also granted a year at the Spanish Riding School, back in Vienna.

Following a decline of royal interest in riding, Seunig became Chief Riding Master of the Yugoslavian Cavalry School in 1930. However, when offered promotion to General, he retired instead, since this would have entailed active service for a country for which he had no patriotic feelings.

After this retirement he kept riding, and, an Olympic competitor himself, also coached the German team that was successful in the Berlin Olympics. When, during the Second World War, Slovenian partisans destroyed his home, he moved to Germany where he gained high office as an equestrian instructor in the army.

After the war, he travelled extensively and became renowned as a rider, teacher and international judge. A great lover of literature, Seunig was also a keen artist and many of his own drawings adorn his books.

Steinbrecht, Gustav (1808–1885) Born in Saxony, Steinbrecht studied veterinary medicine before becoming a pupil of Louis

Seeger, one of the most influential trainers of the nineteenth century, who had, himself, been a pupil of Weyrother, a celebrated figure of the Spanish Riding School.

Steinbrecht stayed with Seeger for eight years, during which time he married Seeger's niece and became an accomplished écuyer. He then took over direction of a manège in Magdeburg, where he remained for a further eight years, before rejoining Seeger.

In 1849, Steinbrecht became director of Seeger's establishment and, at about this time, began to make the notes that were to form the basis of *The Gymnasium of the Horse*. Seeger himself disagreed with the teachings of François Baucher – also active at this time – preferring methods and principles expounded by de la Guérinière. That Steinbrecht shared Seeger's view of Baucher is obvious from the vigorous attacks upon Baucher's method which permeate *The Gymnasium of the Horse*.

As Steinbrecht's health failed, he entrusted the completion of his book to his pupil/disciple, Paul Plinzer. Through Plinzer, and Plinzer's eminent pupil, Hans von Heydebreck, the work of Steinbrecht had a major influence on the formulation of the German [army] Riding Rules, and on German equitation in general.

Wätjen, Richard L. Born in 1891, early backing from his parents enabled Wätjen to embark upon a career devoted entirely to equitation – and he did not squander this privileged position. After studying at Trakehen and Graditz, both German government studs, he spent six years (1916–21) as a pupil of the Spanish Riding School, then stayed on for a further six years as a guest amateur instructor and trainer.

In 1925, he moved to Berlin and began training horses and riders on a professional basis. This scheme proved highly successful: his pupils achieved great national and international success, and he was instrumental in training several Olympic teams, including the British team which competed at Helsinki in 1952.

As a rider, he produced many horses of various breeds to the highest standards, and achieved international success competing in both dressage and showjumping, two of his best-known horses being Burgsdorff and Wotan. Many authorities regard him as being one of the most elegant riders of his era.

Winnett, John Born in Los Angeles in 1928, Winnett was educated in Paris, where he was introduced to riding in the French classical tradition by Victor Laurent, a retired officer from Saumur who had studied under the doctrine of L'Hotte. Winnett subsequently became interested in showjumping and was instructed according to the methods of Col. Danloux, who had refined principles introduced by Federico Caprilli. He became French Junior National Champion in 1945.

As an adult Winnett 'abandoned serious riding to pursue a career' in the Indian sub-continent, Europe and subsequently New York. This 'abandonment' did not prevent him from amateur race-riding, playing polo and, indeed, representing the USA in the 1952 World Showjumping Championships.

Retiring early from a successful career, Winnett turned his full concentration upon horses and went to Germany, to study with Reiner Klimke. In Germany, he was initially surprised to discover a very free-moving style of equitation which traced back to the teachings of de la Guérinière. Much influenced by these German methods, to which he added a detailed study of equine biomechanics, Winnett achieved great success in competition dressage, becoming riding captain of the American team at the 1972 Olympics and continuing to represent his country at the highest levels throughout the 1970s and 1980s.

Wynmalen, Henry (1889–1964) Undoubtedly one of the most influential figures in British equitation, Wynmalen was Dutch by birth and spent his early life in Holland, coming to England in 1927. An engineer by profession, Wynmalen's many interests included yachting, motor rallying and aviation. A flying accident, which left a legacy of back trouble, resulted in Wynmalen adopting a somewhat individualistic riding posture, but did not prevent him from being a consummate all-round horseman.

His early years were devoted primarily to showjumping, cross-country riding and racing, and he was, for many years, MFH to the Woodland Hunt. Always concerned with the correct schooling of horses, and renowned for his quiet, patient methods, he became increasingly interested in classical dressage. In 1948, he won the British Dressage Championship, and followed this with many other successes. His displays at the Royal Windsor Show, and the ease with which his 'dressage' horses performed across country, served to ignite a greater interest in dressage in Britain – an interest he helped to promote with no reduction in his enthusiasm for the other disciplines.

A highly successful breeder and exhibitor of show horses, a respected judge and President of the Arab Horse Society, Wynmalen also served on the Executive Council of the BHS. Largely responsible for organising the horse trials competition at the 1948 (London) Olympics, he played a major role in instigating one-day events and, for some years, served as President of the Jury at Badminton horse trials.